SEA MORE: CARIBBEAN

GET THE MOST OUT OF YOUR DAY IN PORT

Former Cruise Ship Crew Member

Valerie D. Perry

FREE GIFT

Download **"Sea More: Bermuda"** FREE

As a special thanks for downloading my book, I'd like to give you a copy of the Bermuda edition completely FREE.

Visit

theroadlotstraveled.com/bermuda-free-gif/

to get your copy today!

To my parents.

Thanks for your constant love and encouragement.

Sorry I keep doing crazy things that scare you-

like running off to work on a cruise ship.

TABLE OF CONTENTS

INTRODUCTION

When you take a cruise you only have a limited amount of time in port. Do you know the best places to eat and shop? The best activities on the islands? What to not waste your time with? If you want to know, keep reading.

This book is for people who want the basics of what to expect in each port and want to learn how to get the most out of their limited time ashore. This is not a comprehensive account of every restaurant and shop on each island. It doesn't list every excursion offered by your ship. But it does provide you with first person advice from first hand experience.

I spent nearly four years as a crew member aboard the Royal Caribbean fleet. I have been on over 130 cruises and a majority of my time was spent in the Caribbean. I have been to some of these islands dozens of times. I, of course, found my favorite places and came back again and again. In this book I will reveal what they are and what makes them so great. I've explored the port towns and sampled the tours. I'll tell you my favorites and what fell short of my expectations.

Whether you are considering taking a cruise, just booked your first cruise, or return to the Caribbean every year, my goal is to help you have a more successful, less stressful day in port. Your cruise vacation should be a fun-filled trip of adventure. This book is here to take the guesswork out of where to go and what to do.

As a crew member, I would tell my friends going ashore with me to "get ready to work." They were always welcome to come along, but I could typically see more in a day than most people would see in a weekend or maybe even a week. As my friend Miguel recently recounted, "We would all get off the ship together, but if we decided to stay in the restaurant and use the wifi all day you would say, 'Adios amigios,' and go off like Dora the Explorer on an adventure!"

I'd like for you to have equally productive time in port. You've spent a lot of money on your cruise so don't waste your time and risk disappointment by wandering into the first restaurant you see or stopping at the first beach you encounter.

Don't take another trip to the Caribbean without reading this book. Some of the greatest memories of my life happened on the islands to which you are heading. I'd like to help you create a trip of a lifetime.

Sail on!

DISCLAIMER

The information you are about to read comes from my personal experiences. I cannot guarantee your experience will be the same. We all have different definitions of "fun" and different expectations for our vacations. Nonetheless, I think everyone sailing to the Caribbean can benefit from reading this book.

None of the restaurants or tours have paid to be included. As a crew member, I frequently received standard crew member discounts at a variety of establishments. I also worked closely with the Shore Excursion Team on my ships and I frequently received discounted or free tours in exchange for a post-tour review with the onboard team - kind of like secret shopping. However, none of the tour operators donated tours or services to be included in this book.

As I noted earlier, I was an employee of Royal Caribbean. While the port information will apply to anyone who visits these islands, any information I give about the ship or its policies may not apply to every cruise line. Always check with the staff of your cruise.

These are just my experiences: the good, the letdowns, and the "I miss it everyday"s. Some of the adventures I had were dangerous and physically demanding. I'm not recommending that anyone duplicate my every move. Evaluate the risks, use common sense, and stay safe. Plan ahead and have a great trip!

SETTING SAIL

"So this is my new home," I thought as I rode in a bus full of strangers. We had just rounded the bend at the end of the Bayonne, New Jersey cruise pier, and Royal Caribbean's Explorer of the Seas was outside my window. I had never seen a cruise ship before this moment. My uncle saw one the week before I was to report to the Explorer and he called me and said, "If you ever get bored, just paint the thing." He was right. This ship was massive.

I got out of the bus and followed everyone into a tent on the pier. The tent had an astroturf floor, empty metal bleachers on one side, a few staffed tables, several telephones for international calls, and lots of crew members and their luggage. I had to present my medical papers to the ship's medical team at one of the tables and they cleared me for boarding.

I crossed the gangway for the first time and loaded my way-too-full suitcase into an x-ray machine. After my luggage was cleared, I temporarily abandoned it near the staircase as I was ushered into another room where I was handed a pile of paperwork. Mid-completion I was introduced to my new manager. He had coke-bottle glasses, a few missing teeth, and looked at my chest as he spoke.

What had I done? I left everything familiar behind, put a few (and yet far too many) possessions in a suitcase, and ran out into the world looking for an adventure. Despite this rocky start to my cruise career, the next four years were life changing. I used to describe my job as "Getting paid to be on vacation" and it truly did feel like that most of the time. I was tan for the first time in my life. I saw clear blue water that I thought existed exclusively in movies. I traveled to places that I only knew of as *The Price is Right* prize destinations. Cruising changed my life.

If you're a first time or inexperienced cruiser, let me cover a few of the basics:

When you take a cruise, you have a limited amount of time in port. You can typically go ashore about half an hour after your ship arrives. Don't rush down to the gangway when you see your ship approaching land. Instead, give the crew a few extra minutes to secure the ship, get the gangway in place, and complete any paperwork required by the local authorities. Typically, an announcement will be made over the ship's PA system when you can disembark ("leave," for all you non-cruisers).

> BONUS ADVICE: Many of the ship's announcements won't come through the speaker in your stateroom. This way the PA won't disturb anyone who may be sleeping and you won't be inundated with information you simply don't care about. The announcements will be broadcast to all public areas, including the hallway outside your stateroom, so just crack the door open to listen.

The All On Board time really does mean all passengers on board at that time. A ship will leave you behind. Cruise lines have a schedule to keep and it's sometimes further complicated by tides and port traffic. Ships need to leave on time. Be back before All On Board or be prepared to pay for a flight to the next island to meet up with the ship again. The ship's port agent can help guests left behind with those arrangements.

This is where shore excursions offered by your ship come in. If you are on a ship sponsored tour and the entire tour group is late, the ship will wait for you. If you went out, hired a taxi or rented a car, incurred a delay and are late, the ship won't wait. That's the main benefit of taking one of the ship's tours. If you want the most stress-free vacation possible, take a tour from the ship. If you want a cheaper alternative and are confident you can return before the All On Board time, set out on your own. In the coming chapters I will recommend some tours that your ship may offer and some others you may have to complete on your own. A little pre-planning, common sense, and good time management will get you back on time.

The Caribbean is a shopping mecca. The tax and duty free status of the islands makes it a great time to stock up on alcohol, electronics, and jewelry. Your ship's Port and Shopping Guide can help you with all of the applicable customs info so you'll be able to get your purchases back into your home country with no issues. The most valuable advice this crew member will give you is, "If you see it and you like it, buy it." The next port may not have what you saw in the first port so if you see something you really like, act on it. A word of caution though, your Port and Shopping Guide gets paid a commission from the stores he or she recommends. You do get benefits from shopping at those stores - such as the guarantee they offer and the free delivery to the ship - but make sure you're getting exactly what you want. They will claim to know what the next big trend will be and that there is a One Week Only deal in certain stores. Chances are that it's not so much a new trend, but rather a product with a high profit margin. And I heard the same speech given week after week advertising the One Week Only deals. Despite these minor inconveniences, you really will find some great deals. I bought electronics, watches, and jewelry during my time in the Caribbean. I recommend making a list before your trip of what you want to buy and what you're willing to pay for it. That way you'll be able to take advantage of the great deals without being swayed by any sales tactics.

If you plan on doing some shopping in port, notify your credit card company before you go. If you haven't traveled recently and there is suddenly a large charge on your card from a jewelry store in the Caribbean, your credit card company could (and should) put a hold on your card. A simple phone call ahead of time could save you a lot of hassle.

If you prefer to pay in cash, most islands will accept United States currency. Be prepared to receive change in the local currency. It's a good idea to check with your Port and Shopping Guide, or the salesperson you're doing business with ashore, to confirm if US currency will be accepted.

With some basic information out of the way, let's cruise!

NASSAU

Only a quick trip from Florida, many cruises call on Nassau. In fact, if you're looking to just give cruising a try, look for short sailings from the ports of Cape Canaveral, Fort Lauderdale, or Miami that will sail out for a day or two in the Bahamas and then back.

BONUS ADVICE: You can predict the demographic a cruise caters to based on its length. Long cruises (14 days or longer) will most likely host an older crowd: people who are retired and don't have to worry about pulling their kids out of school for a few weeks. The shortest cruises (3-4 days) will host the party crowd: people who are looking to get out of town for a long weekend and, in many cases, drink and party their worries away. Families heavily populate the medium length cruises (5-12 days) with a spike in attendance over the summer and around all of the school holidays. Of course, these can always vary, but keep this in mind when booking your trip.

Located on the Bahamian island of New Providence, the city of Nassau has a lot to offer. There are stores, beaches, and restaurants close to the cruise ship pier. Nassau offers something for everyone.

Many of the ship's top excursions will be taking guests to Atlantis. The resort of Atlantis can be seen across the water from where the cruise ships dock. It's landmark coral colored buildings on Paradise Island tower over the landscape. Atlantis is beautiful and remarkable, but be prepared to pay. Atlantis is so close and accessible to the ship that you can easily do an excursion there on your own. Do some research before your cruise, find pricing of the activity you'd like to try, and compare it with the ship's pricing. You'll likely save some money, but you are now also responsible for making it back to the ship on time.

There is no charge to enter the resort so consider taking a cab or the water taxi over if you just want to have a look around. The options will be limited in terms of how far you can go without buying a ticket and getting a wristband. They have a large security team and you will get stopped if you try to go somewhere you're not allowed. And yes, I'm speaking from experience. The free area includes the casino so you can stop by and make a donation. There is also a nice, new shopping and dining area located along the marina. It is a great area to stroll through, grab a snack, and drool at the yachts.

I bought a pass to the aquarium during one visit. It's one of the largest aquariums I've been to and many of the glass cases are open at the top for two views: one from the halls of the aquarium and another from along the sidewalks outside. Everything was very well designed and it was such an immersive experience that I found it hard to believe I was still in the Bahamas and not transported to the lost city of Atlantis. If you have ever visited Las Vegas, this is the Vegas casino of aquariums. It's all very over the top, incredible, and completely worth the visit.

The Atlantis waterpark is amazing as well. It offers many unique experiences; from a lengthy lazy river to a water slide through a shark filled aquarium. They even have a not so lazy river: a mile long ride filled with rapids, splashes, and fun.

The beaches at Atlantis also require a fee, but there is a free beach nearby. Ask your taxi driver to take you to Cabbage Beach. The beaches I visited were on the edge of downtown Nassau. I walked off the ship and headed through the terminal towards downtown. Once outside, I turned right and walked along the water. At a certain point the oceanfront sidewalk stops and I had to cut in a few streets and go through a parking lot, but I could see the water most of the time and just kept following the shoreline. Soon I reached an extensive span of beaches. Compared to other islands, these beaches were nothing remarkable, but they were convenient.

If you decide to take this route and walk around Nassau, use caution. According to the United States State Department, there has been a spike in criminal activity and the criminal threat level is critical. I never had any problems here (or anywhere, really), but be careful. A mugging would put a dark cloud over your vacation. Check out the Safety Tips later in this book.

While downtown, take a couple hours to check out The Pirates Museum. It may not look like much from the outside, but this museum is deceptively large and my visit exceeded my expectations. The first exhibit hall features a Caribbean street from 1716 and a full-size pirate ship. Next, I was inside the ship for a firsthand look at the living quarters. The museum also features exhibits that outline the history of pirates in the Caribbean. I highly recommend this museum to anyone with an interest in pirates or history or looking for an educational alternative to the beach.

On one of my early trips to Nassau a friend asked me if I wanted to go dance with flamingos. Confused, I said, "Um, what?" He explained that there was a place outside of Nassau where you can enter an arena with the birds and they run around while you get your photo taken with them. It sounded intriguing, so I went along. Ardastra Gardens had more to offer than just flamingos, they basically have a small zoo. As we walked around we kept calling it a "homemade zoo." It didn't look like a zoo you would find in the States and none of the cages looked particularly sturdy. Some were just wire fencing stretched over a wooden frame. According to their website Ardastra Gardens, Zoo, and Conservation Center does a lot of work to protect animals and educate the public on conservation matters.

Seeing the flamingos was fun, but they don't exactly dance. There is a drill sergeant type person who gets in the ring with them. He yells and blows a whistle and the birds run around and reverse their direction. At the end of the show we each got a chance to get in the ring and stand still as the birds ran around. It's definitely as close as I've ever gotten to a flamingo. We all took turns snapping photos of each other amongst the birds and those pictures are some of my favorite souvenirs.

SHOPPING

Nassau is a great shopping port. They have all of the standard Caribbean stores you will begin to recognize throughout the islands. Steps from the ship you'll find Diamonds International, Colombian Emeralds International, Del Sol, and so many more. Most of the stores here are quite large so you'll find a good selection. Make this one of your main shopping days.

DINING

Dunkin' Donuts - Across the street from The Pirates Museum, Dunkin' Donuts is just like what you are used to back home. So rejoice, New Englanders! Your coffee of choice is on tap. This Dunkin' Donuts is where I once ate a bacon and egg breakfast sandwich on a sliced glazed doughnut instead of toast or a biscuit. Terribly unhealthy to be sure, but actually quite tasty.

Hard Rock Café - As another chain, it's similar to what you would find in other locations. Hard Rock is located in the middle of town and makes an opportune lunch stop.

Pirate's Pub - Conveniently located right downtown and next to The Pirates Museum, Pirate's Pub has good food and wifi in a sports bar atmosphere.

PERFECT DAY

Nassau is compact enough to do it all. I'd get off the ship early and hit the shops. Bring the purchases back on board or have the ship's Port and Shopping Guide deliver them and head out for an afternoon at Atlantis, the beach, or The Pirates Museum. Back on board, find a chair on an outer deck for sailaway. Ships sail right past Nassau Harbour Lighthouse for the perfect backdrop of last minute photos.

BELOW DECK: MY JOB

My official job title was "Broadcast Technician." I would simplify it to "I do video work" to help my friends back home understand how I spent my time. In reality, my role encompassed a lot.

My team was responsible for all of the content on the televisions around the ship. Sometimes that meant tuning in satellite signals or loading and monitoring digital media players or even filming and editing commercials or full-length shows. We recorded some of the entertainment in the theater, game shows, and a talk show with the Cruise Director.

We scheduled and monitored the on board cinema and provided video support to live theater shows when necessary. We all carried phones and were on call 24/7. If a movie wasn't playing right, a guest had a question about the television programing, or a television in a bar wasn't playing what the guests or the bartenders wanted, we got a call and were expected to respond immediately.

Our main project each cruise was filming and editing the souvenir DVD that the guests could purchase. This DVD contained some stock segments such as an interview with the Captain, port information, and a tour of the ship, but it also contained several segments that were reshot every single cruise to feature the new guests. Filming for this project was one of my favorite parts of my job. I loved being out and around the ship, filming people having the time of their lives on vacation. That's a big part of why I used to say, "I get paid to be on vacation." Even though I was working, I was having so much fun and surrounded by so many happy people that it rarely felt like work.

COZUMEL

Every crew member's dream port, Cozumel has it all: amazing restaurants, great shopping, and pristine beaches. There are a few different piers in Cozumel. I typically docked at International Pier which isn't directly downtown, but there are plenty of taxis available and the ride is less than ten minutes. I frequently walked back and forth to town.

Everything is so accessible that I only did a couple tours through the ship. The first tour was when my sister cruised and we did the dolphin swim at Dolphin Discovery. In Cozumel, the tour groups don't meet immediately off the ship like they do in most other ports. Instead we had to walk down the pier and through a gate into a shopping plaza where all of the tour operators were standing with signs for their tours. From there we were loaded into taxis and whisked away for our adventure.

I hadn't read the brochure closely to know what we were in for, I simply told the on board Shore Excursions Team that we wanted to swim with dolphins. I was pleasantly surprised when we got there to learn that our tour included not only a swim session with dolphins, but also an encounter with a manatee. In fact, it was called "Dolphin Push, Pull & Swim with Manatee Interaction." The day began with a safety briefing, but not for our safety; for our dolphin's safety. The trainers had a small, plush dolphin and they showed us where we should and should not touch the real dolphins.

When it was time to get in the water, our group of about 10 people climbed down the stairs and onto a metal platform that had us chest deep in the cold ocean. Then we got to meet our dolphin, Mauricio. He swam by multiple times and we got to touch him. I have touched dolphins at SeaWorld before, but this was the first time I was in the water with one (they frown on that at SeaWorld).

Our first activity was the push. We were given a boogie board to lay on and were told to keep our feet together and our legs straight. Mauricio circled around me, put his nose on my foot, and pushed me across the enclosure. For some reason I was surprised that the dolphin only put his nose on my one foot. I don't know why that surprised me, it's not like he has two noses, but it did. The only semi-scary part of the whole thing is that we were going so fast I was concerned that Mauricio was trying to make a break for it by pushing me through the end of the enclosure. But he wasn't and we stopped with plenty of room to spare.

After all the other members of our group completed the push, it was time for the pull. I was told to float upright in the water, raise my right hand above my head, and put my left hand on my chest. Mauricio swam behind me and flipped over on his back. As he swam under my raised arm, I grabbed his pectoral fins and we glided through the water. It was so much fun!

We completed a few other activities like giving the dolphin a kiss and getting a dolphin kiss. We had a water fight wherein we splashed Mauricio and he "splashed" us back. They may call it "splashing," but I call it "spitting" and wasn't very excited when the dolphin spit went in my mouth. However, a lot of seawater has been in my mouth over the years and I know there must be dolphin spit and whole lot more in there.

I had waited until my final contract to swim with the dolphins and it was worth the wait. They are majestic and beautiful creatures and it was an honor to share the water with them for a short while. The only downside to this tour is that cameras are not permitted for the safety of the animals. A photographer from the resort was on hand and our pictures were available for purchase in the gift shop at the end of the tour.

After our dolphin swim we were led down another pier where we got in the water with a manatee. The interaction with the manatees is limited so we were only permitted to pet them. As my sister said, "It feels like a hairy potato." It really did! When else are you going to get the chance to pet a manatee?

Dolphin Discovery is within Chakanaab National Park and our tour included access to the park's other amenities. First we headed to the sea lion show. The wooden bleachers in the amphitheater lack comfort and quickly get crowded. However, the show is incredibly entertaining so it's worth it. After laughing at the antics of these friendly creatures, I went down to the beach for some snorkeling. The good snorkel sites were pretty crowded the day we were there, but I was still able to see lots of undersea life. While I was snorkeling, my sister headed to the Tequila Factory for a look through the museum and a tasting.

Chakannaab is a destination all on it's own. We only saw a tiny portion of what this park has to offer and I would like to go back and spend more time. Your ship will likely offer a tour there, but consider booking this one yourself if you are comfortable managing your time and taking a taxi on your own. Current pricing is available on the Chakannaab website and they sometimes post discount coupons.

Return cab fare was also included in our tour package. Cabs were running all day and we just needed to line up where our cab had dropped us off when we were ready. The cabs go to whatever destination is requested; typically back to the ship or downtown.

The other tour I took was a stingray swim at Stingray Beach called Everybody Loves Rays! They get bonus points for a clever name. I was a bit nervous about this tour, but the barbs are trimmed so I had nothing to worry about. It was completely safe.

The tour began with a stingray information session, safety briefing, and snorkeling instruction. We then got into the deep water and swam and snorkeled with our guides as they pointed out stingrays and other marine life. The photos I have from this tour are amazing! There were stingrays everywhere and I was able to get some great shots. In addition, I gave my camera to one of the guides who dove down for even better angles.

It was then time for us to get into the shallow water, feed the stingrays, and hold them as we posed for photos. This was another great opportunity to face my fears and try something new. These creatures are silky smooth and surprisingly strong! It was an incredible experience to be a part of their world for a while. No cameras were permitted in this shallow water portion, but they had a photographer on hand to snap photos of us with the stingrays. These photos are, of course, available for purchase at the end of the tour. The photos come on a disc with all of the photos from the session plus some postcard quality images. If you are in a big group, you can plan to just buy a disc or two and share the pictures.

After the swim I hung out, had lunch, and met some of the other creatures they have on hand. My favorite was the iguana who was missing a foot. He sat on my head as we posed for a photograph. Hello, next year's Christmas card!

While I only booked those two tours through the ship, I completed a few on my own. The most ambitious was a drive around the entire island with my parents. We rented a "Mexican Convertible" (as the salesman called it) from a rental location on the outskirts of the port. It was a small SUV with the top cut off and a retrofitted, removable canvas roof. We had a little trouble finding the road that allowed us to cut through town to the other side of the island, so make sure you get a map and clear directions.

I had never been anywhere on the island aside from the port, downtown, and the small area in between. I was very surprised to find the opposite side much more rugged and windier than my usual side. Although Cozumel was already one of my favorite ports, its favor grew in my heart that day. A short drive to the other side of the island had us out of the crowds and surrounded by nature.

Much of the drive took us between the coast and a vast green expanse of island countryside. We found many spots for great photo ops along the wind-blown coast. The jagged rocks, the roaring waves, and endless green vegetation had us thinking we'd been transported to another country. It looks completely different from the port side of Cozumel. Keep a watchful eye open for iguanas as you may find them crossing the road and ducking into the tall grass.

We cut through the island first, then south and around. Our first stop was Coconuts. This place has a beach bar feel, but is more accurately described as a cliff bar. It sits high atop a hill that plunges into the sea. The view is spectacular. There are winding walkways and multiple seating areas. Stop in and say hello to several tropical birds that call Coconuts home.

From there we made several photo stops along the beach before a stop at the souvenir shops near Celarain Lighthouse on the south point. We considered a trip out to Celarain Lighthouse and Punta Sur park, but the entrance fee kept us away. It was $14 per person and we knew we didn't have much time. We had more than enough free things to see. Punta Sur is gorgeous and deserves a day to itself, so we'll save it for another visit.

We made a stop for lunch at Playa Palancar. This resort is beautiful. The food is nothing fancy, but the view is incredible. Be warned: the dirt road back to the resort can be an adventure. Four-wheel drive isn't necessary, but you will get jostled. Think of it as a free massage. We didn't have time to snorkel or try any of the other amenities here. We just got a snack, relaxed a bit, and got back on the road.

The next stop took us inland, away from the beach, to the Mayan ruins of El Cedral. This is a small site, but a great way to add Mayan ruins to the list of things you saw in Cozumel. Consider booking a more robust tour through your ship if you are interested in ruins or Mayan culture. Many ships will even offer tours that take guests to Tulum on the mainland for larger Mayan ruins.

Our final stop before heading back to the ship was Playa Corona, or Corona Beach. We were told about this place from the man who rented us the car. It's not far from the ship, but I had never heard of it. Playa Corona isn't much to look at. A little shack with plastic patio furniture along a crumbling sea wall is all you'll find here. I was told the snorkeling was good, but I was skeptical of this place based on appearance. I was pleasantly surprised as the snorkeling here was spectacular. The sea was rough so it was more physically demanding than most snorkel trips, but we were the only people in the water so it was worth the effort. The variety of coral and other sea life rivals what I've experienced on other islands throughout the Caribbean. My favorite find was a barracuda who studied me from afar. We ended our day with a soda at Playa Corona before returning the car to the port.

BONUS ADVICE: Stay on "Ship's Time." Ship's Time is the time it is onboard and this may or may not match what time it is on shore or even what time it is on other ships in the same port. If you are on a cruise sailing from Florida you are starting your vacation in the Eastern Time Zone. Some islands operate on Eastern time, but some operate on Atlantic time. To complicate matters further, this changes throughout the year. To simplify the process the cruise industry came up with the idea of "Ship's Time." When you first get onboard, check the time on the telephone in your stateroom and set your watch to match. This is the official time. Multiple announcements will be made if you ever need to adjust this time. It's always a good idea to double check the ship's phone and your watch before heading ashore to make sure you won't miss All On Board. Never rely on the time on your cell phone or ask a local for the time. I thankfully never missed the ship, but I was once late for work because I didn't observe Ship's Time.

During my final months at sea, my friends started hanging out at a resort a bit further down the coast from Playa Corona called Paradise Beach. This is another place that has it all. Guests can lay on the beach, snorkel, swim in the pool, or grab lunch or a cocktail. This place was typically busy, but not overcrowded. The snorkeling is much better at Playa Corona, but the rest of the facilities are nicer here. We actually spent a lot of our time in and around the pool where we could enjoy the sun, warmth, and water within striking distance of the bar and without the nuisance of sand.

Paradise Beach and Playa Corona are both within biking distance of the ship. Exit the port area, turn right, keep following the water, and you'll eventually find them. Much of the trip is on a paved bike path and some is on a less traveled back road, so it's a great route for even inexperienced road bikers. To be honest, I hadn't been on a bike in years when I tried this trip and my friend that came with me had quite the night of partying and very little sleep. If we can do it, you can do it.

The place where I spent a majority of my time in Cozumel is, hands-down, No Name Bar. No Name is a crew bar on land. It's not the place for the older crowd or families, but if you're young and looking for a good time, check it out. It's located just over halfway between the pier and the heart of downtown. It makes a great final stop on your way back to the ship.

No Name is known for its affordable drinks, swim up bar, and casual atmosphere. It's common to see crew jumping off the pier and swimming out to a floating white platform. The water is so clear that a sunken airplane on the ocean floor is visible while sitting on that platform.

Some of my favorite memories from all of my contracts involve doing a tequila shot, climbing the narrow sea wall, and jumping out over the rocks into the ocean. Although I can't recommend this, there was something exhilarating about facing my fears and sharing this experience with my friends. After I made the jump and was in the water I realized that was the easy part. The hard part was fighting the current and swimming over to the steps.

Whatever you decide to do, leave yourself enough time to get back to the ship. The line at security on the pier can get crazy leading up to All On Board. The trouble only compounds if there are multiple ships at your pier. And pay attention to the signs at security. There are typically separate lines for separate ships.

SHOPPING

You'll find many of the Caribbean standards. One notable exception is Los Cinco Soles. This place has lots of great Mexican souvenirs, tequila, and other mementos. One of my favorite shops is Mayan Fiesta Rum Cakes. Stop in for rum cake samples and take a look at The Wall of Fire. The Wall of Fire is an entire side of the shop dedicated to Mexican hot sauces. Don't go home empty handed.

DINING

Guidos- I'll admit it; it's a bit strange to go for Italian food in Mexico. But if Mexican just isn't your cuisine of choice, give this downtown place a try. Everything I had here was amazing. The portions are huge and you won't leave hungry.

La Choza – My top pick for Cozumel. La Choza is located on a back street and although I've been there multiple times, I still have a hard time finding it. So consider taking a cab. Just say "La Choza" and the driver will know what to do. Everything here is amazing. The La Choza sauce may be the best thing you eat all cruise. Even better, you can buy bottles of it to take home with you. In fact, if any of you head there after reading this, feel free to pick me up a bottle. You are immediately served nachos and La Choza sauce. It may be hard to control yourself, but save some room for other dishes. My favorite is actually the loaded nachos with chicken or steak. Everything I tried here over the years has been excellent.

Pancho's Backyard- Located next to Los Cinco Soles, you won't find a more convenient place for lunch during a shopping trip. The atmosphere in this outdoor courtyard is delightful. There is typically a live band playing and the tables are spread out with trees and other vegetation separating them. It's actually a huge place, and it is so spacious that it never felt crowded. Pancho's has an extensive margarita menu. I tried a few of them and loved each one.

Rock 'n Java- If you're heading off the ship early, consider stopping by Rock 'n Java for breakfast. I highly recommend the croissant sandwiches and milkshakes. Yes, milkshakes for breakfast. Why not? You're on vacation!

PERFECT DAY

If I'm feeling active I would probably bike over to Playa Corona and snorkel for awhile. The other side of the island is another must see for anyone who has already experienced downtown. My standard go to was a long lunch at La Choza, an afternoon relaxing at No Name Bar, and a long walk back to the ship to walk off some of what I consumed that day.

BELOW DECK: A TYPICAL DAY

Based on my Facebook and blog posts, most of my friends back home thought that living on a ship consisted exclusively of sitting on beaches and exploring exotic destinations. They weren't completely wrong, but there is more to it than that.

First of all, I had one of the best jobs with the nicest schedules on board. As a Broadcast Technician, I didn't have many responsibilities while the ship was in port. There was the occasional maintenance day where I stayed on board and worked with my team to repair equipment, but for the most part I was free when we were docked.

I made up for all that freedom on the days the ship was at sea. There were days I began work at 8:00 am or earlier and worked pretty much straight through until midnight or later. Most of those hours were by choice though. My actual schedule from my supervisor typically only listed three or four hours of work. However, I preferred to work straight through the sea days, get everything done, and enjoy my time in port.

On a day at sea I would wake up with enough time to get ready for my first event. As I said, sometimes this was at 8:00 or earlier, but it was usually around 10:00 or 11:00. I'd film an event or two then take a lunch break. After lunch I would film more events or edit in the Broadcast Room until dinner. After dinner I would switch into evening attire and probably work another event or two and get some more editing done. The last event of the day sometimes did not begin until 11:45 pm.

On a port day I would try to get off the ship at 10:00 and not return until 30-60 minutes before "All On Board" or my first scheduled event. I may have had an event or two in the evening, but working only a few hours on a port day was pretty standard for me.

It depended on the ship and the team, but overall I had a very flexible and easy schedule. I was able to get my work done when it was convenient for me and spend the rest of the time exploring.

JAMAICA

Cruise ships dock in Ocho Rios and Falmouth, Jamaica. Both towns are on the northern coast of the island. Falmouth is home to a recently constructed mega-pier to service the largest ships afloat today. It has a developing port area with brick sidewalks lined with shops and restaurants. Falmouth also has a row of great informational signs that tell the history of Jamaica and this area. The signs are still inside the gate of the port area, but are towards downtown.

Regardless of where you dock, Jamaica is another great tour day. The immediate port areas of both towns are fairly safe and secure, but use caution if you venture out into the actual towns. On one of my first trips to Falmouth, I decided to walk around town, check things out, and find a restaurant with wifi. I took a fifteen-minute walk through the center of town. I walked down a side street and saw a restaurant and bar in a large parking lot. Many of the customers looked like crew members (not many guests spend their vacation in a Caribbean island on laptops). I walked in and found a seat. When no one came to take my order I walked up to the bar. Chatting with the bartender and a local was one of the singers on the ship, Lucas, who I recognized, but hadn't met yet. I saw this as a good sign that this must be a good place. He worked in my division on board, we shared a lot of friends, and he was here, so it must be good. Right? He recognized me too and said hello. As I was ordering he said he was getting ready to go and asked if I wanted to walk back to the ship with him. What? That's weird. I don't even know this guy and I just got here. Why was he asking me to go back with him?

I saw Lucas later that night back on board. He came up to me in the crew mess and told me he didn't feel safe at that restaurant so he asked me to come with him to get me out of there. I totally missed that signal. He told me that the local he had been talking to at the bar was very friendly and walked out with him. He walked Lucas through town, but when they were approaching the gate to the port the man turned to him and said, "Give me $40." Lucas laughed. But then he looked at the man's face. He was completely serious. Lucas said, "I only have $20." He gave the man the money and he walked off. I guess it's a good thing I didn't go with him. It was an inadvertent invitation to get robbed. I never had any problems in any of the ports I visited, but use caution. Check out the Safety Tips at the end of this book for some helpful information.

Ocho Rios and Falmouth are not too far apart, so most of the tours go to the same places. The tours offered through the ship will be similar from both towns. I tried a number of these tours.

One very specific tour was the Royal 5K. This race was offered through select Royal Caribbean ships and featured a course that wove its way through Falmouth and along the coast. Participating in the race allowed me to see many "slice of life" situations throughout Jamaica that I wouldn't have seen on other tours. If you're a runner this is a great way to take in some sights on your vacation while burning off a bit of the buffet. The Royal 5K has only been offered a few times and I haven't heard an official word on if it will be offered again.

Many of the ship's tours are run through a local company called Chukka. When my parents cruised they opted to do Chukka's Good Hope Estate and Plantation tour. I'll be completely honest: I was skeptical about this tour. I'm always up for adventure, but touring an old house did not sound exciting to me. It's not something I would have chosen for myself, but I'm so glad they did because I loved it!

We met our tour group off the ship in the designated area and we loaded in vans for the transport to Chukka. We were given a quick tour around an old pottery studio before we loaded into a truck to explore the plantation grounds. Our guides told us some history of Jamaica and the plantation, explained what was grown here, and even let us try some of the blood oranges. We caught a glimpse of an elusive mongoose while in the orchard and we made a photo stop at an old water wheel.

After a thorough tour of the grounds and lots of new information in our heads, we returned back to where our tour began for a lunch of jerk chicken. Just like this tour, I didn't think I would like jerk chicken. I was wrong a lot that day! The tour we booked included this delicious lunch. Check with your ship's Shore Excursion Team for details on the tours they offer.

After lunch it was time to check out the Good Hope Estate mansion. We were walked through by a guide who told us all about the previous owners, the history of Good Hope, and related it to the history of Jamaica. We learned that this home had running water before New York City. There was time at the end of the tour to ask questions and a bit of free time to explore the grounds on our own and take photos.

On one of my last cruises, my roommate and I took an ATV tour with Chukka. Full ATV operating instructions were given and no prior experience was necessary. We were in a small group of about ten people and soon we all donned our helmets, jumped on our ATVs, and took off on a guided tour of the Jamaican countryside. One guide led the group while another brought up the rear and assisted anyone having a difficult time with their ATV. My roommate and I fell behind when we each stalled, but the rear guide was able to assist us and bring us back to the rest of the group.

We drove through fields and along the coast before stopping along a dirt road for our guide to explain what some of the native Jamaican plants were around us. It was a brief stop so we were quickly back on the trail. We eventually arrived at coastal cliffs and were told we could jump in. As much as I love adventure, I'm afraid of heights and was skeptical of the safety of jumping off a cliff into the ocean. But, my fear motivates me, so in I went.

If you book this tour, bring a towel and a change of clothes. The trail can be muddy and if you decide to jump in the ocean it is a long and soggy trip back to the ship if you are unprepared. No one gave me this advice and I drip-dried the whole way back.

When my sister cruised, we decided to check out one of the most famous sites in Jamaica: Dunn's River Falls. We were feeling adventurous and decided to climb the falls with our group. Like all of the tours, we met our group in the pier area just off the ship and loaded in a van that took us to the falls.

As I mentioned, Dunn's River Falls is one of the most famous sites on the island and it shows; the falls will be crowded if there are multiple ships in Jamaica on the day you visit. There were hundreds of people in multiple groups outside the entrance the day we were there. Listen to your guide, follow him, and try to stick together as you get inside.

Our first stop was at the shoe hut. Everyone climbing the falls must be wearing water shoes. I thought this was just strongly encouraged, but it's actually a requirement. Plan ahead and bring water shoes if you have them. We didn't have our own but we could rent a pair to use for the day or buy a pair to keep.

After our group was looking stylish in our newly rented footwear, we followed our guide along a downhill path and into the ocean at the base of the falls. This is a great time for a photo if you have a waterproof camera. Leave your camera on board if you don't have a waterproof one; you're about to get soaked.

As we approached the falls they made us all hold hands. Personally, I hated this part. I'm a better scrambler than I am walker and I wanted the use of my hands to pull me up and over rocks. Plus, if I fell I didn't want to take other people down with me. Not to mention that I didn't want to be taken down if other people fell. But the amount of people criss-crossing their way up the falls made it necessary to hang on to each other so we wouldn't lose our group.

The guide is at the front and the person behind him is meant to step where he steps. The following person steps where the person in front of them steps and so on and so forth on down the line. I was typically at the end of the line and unfortunately this turns into an exaggerated game of Telephone. Just like the phrase wasn't the same at the end of the line in elementary school, the footing wasn't exactly the same as the guide had intended at the end of the line. I had lots of bumps and bruises from careening off rocks, but no major damage.

The climb is constant and fairly fast. We didn't get any big breaks for a swim or photo ops. We paused briefly for a few people to try out a natural waterslide and another time to "trust fall" into a giant swimming hole. But for the most part we kept moving. There were too many people coming up behind us for us to take too much time. Before I knew it we were at the top and returning our rented shoes.

I'm glad I did the Dunn's River Falls climb as it is the iconic excursion in Jamaica, but I found it stressful. It was very crowded and I felt rushed. I also felt like I didn't really get to see the falls. I was so close I was literally in the waterfall and that's not a good perspective from which to view its total beauty. However, the challenge of climbing the falls left me feeling very accomplished.

The tour we were on included lunch and an afternoon of river tubing. After the falls climb we were taken to a hotel on the beach and greeted with a glass of rum punch upon arrival. The back patio along the ocean was set with a buffet lunch and we dined on pasta, salad, fruit, jerk chicken, and dessert. There were lots of options and no one left hungry.

After lunch we were delivered to a riverside hut. We had a short wait for our tubes as they were being brought up via truck from downstream where another group had just finished using them. We donned our lifejackets and were soon floating along the river.

On the river, we passed locals hanging out on rafts tethered to the shore. We could smell the "Jamaican herbs" they were smoking as we floated past. Yet another slice of life situation, I guess.

The rest of the float trip was uneventful and relaxing. There were a few minor rapids, but nothing crazy. My sister and I easily hung on to each other's tubes throughout much of the trip to stay together.

I took a tour to Cornwall Beach in Montego Bay as part of my quest to complete what I call "The Kokomo Sweep." As defined by the Beach Boys, this includes: Aruba, Jamaica, Bermuda, Bahama, Key Largo, Montego. My trip to Cornwall Beach in Montego Bay got me one step   closer.

I participated in the Irie Mon Beach Party trip and had a great time. The beach was not crowded and chairs and umbrellas were included as was a delicious lunch buffet. There was constant reggae music playing, so this is not a top pick if you are looking for a quiet getaway. But it's a fun atmosphere on a beautiful beach.

In the afternoon the reggae music stopped and an announcer got on the mic and told us it was time for trivia. We didn't need to leave our beach chairs or the water to play. We were instructed to listen to the question and shout out the answer if we knew it. It was unconventional and potentially disruptive to others just trying to relax. I'm pretty sure my friends and I were the only people playing, but we loved it! We worked on cruise ships and had visited a lot of beaches, but this was the only one to offer us trivia. I'm not sure how they kept score, but I won! I still have the plastic cup that was my prize and the magnet stuffed inside it is now proudly displayed on my refrigerator.

Cornwall Beach was great, but Montego Bay is a bit of a haul from Falmouth and even further from Ocho Rios. For ships docked in Falmouth, consider taking the ten-minute ride to Red Stripe Beach. The sand is white, the water is clear, and guests can get lost in this little slice of paradise for a few hours. Take a walk in the shallow water as far as time allows. You'll soon be out of tourist territory and surrounded by beautiful landscapes.

Be sure to check the details of the beach package you purchase. The Cornwall Beach Party included chairs, food, and drinks. But many trips to Red Stripe Beach just include transportation and entrance; chairs, food, and drinks are all extra. Read the brochure closely and ask the staff if you have any questions.

After completing a big project for the Shore Excursion Team on my ship, I was offered a tour of my choice. My choice was easy: I wanted to take the Jamaican Helicopter Tour. I'd never been in a helicopter before that day, but I learned that when you show up with a big camera, people give you a good seat.

The tour met out on the pier, just like all the others. Soon I was in a van and after a short drive through town we arrived at a small building. Obviously a helicopter can only take up a few people at a time so the building was a tiny waiting area where we hung out and waited our turn. I was in the last group, but I got the co-pilot seat, so the wait was worth it. The front seat is the place to be if you can manage it. I had my window, plus the windshield, and there were large glass panels on the floor. I had a much larger range of view than those sitting in the back.

The view from the air was stunning. The trip began with a flight over our ship. I'd been living on that ship for five months and I'd seen it from just about every angle available, but this was a new one for me. After the ship, we cut inland to view some of Jamaica's towns and neighboring wilderness. Each passenger was wearing a headset the entire trip and the pilot was pointing out places of interest. We each had a talkback mic in case we had any questions. It was a pretty quiet trip as we were all too mesmerized by the views to speak.

We flew over Dunn's River Falls, which is hard to see from the air as the canopy of trees obstructs most of the view. I would have missed it if the guide hadn't pointed it out. On the way back we flew along the coast and the bottom of the falls were much easier to spot out there.

The coastal flyover on the return trip was the best part of the entire tour. Jamaica's coastline is gorgeous. I had only seen a couple beaches from the ground and assumed the rest of the island looked similar, but I couldn't have been more wrong. In some areas cliffs covered in green vegetation plunged into the sea. The water was such a clear, brilliant, blue that I saw the reef systems hundreds of feet below us. I had spent years in the Caribbean, but I had never seen it like this.

It's a quick flight. The tour seemed way too short, but it completely changed my view of Jamaica. A helicopter tour is a pricey excursion, but if you feel like you've seen and done all the Caribbean has to offer, take a look at it from above. Something will surprise you.

Nearly all of the tours I took in Jamaica were through the ship, but a couple times my friends wanted to go to The Blue Hole. Information between cruise ship crew members can be a bit like folklore. It's passed down from generation to generation. It's how we find out the must-see spots, the places with the best crew discounts, and where to find the fastest wifi. The Blue Hole topped the list of Jamaica's must-sees.

The Blue Hole is southeast of Ocho Rios. Expect a 15-30 minute drive from Ocho Rios and around a 90 minute drive from Falmouth. I visited the Blue Hole from both ports. When we were coming from Falmouth we added a brief stop at a grocery store in Ocho Rios for some snacks. The best part of the Blue Hole is its natural state. It is completely non-commercialized. However, that means that you need to take everything you will need for the day with you. Nothing is available for purchase. Also be sure to carry everything out with you to protect this beautiful place.

Confirm with your cab what time you will need to be picked up as you are being dropped off. The Blue Hole is in a remote area and cabs do not frequently pass along this route. Since this isn't a tour through your ship, you are solely responsible for getting back on time.

As we were getting out of the cabs several local guides greeted us. These guides stuck with us throughout the day, showed us the best places to jump in, helped guide us down the waterfalls, and reset the rope swing for us. I wouldn't want to try to do this day without a guide. There are hidden rocks under the water and the guides know where it's safe to jump in. It's a good idea to get the price of your day from your guide as you begin so there are no surprises.

> BONUS ADVICE: Pack light. Only take the essentials on your tour. Leave your phones, tablets, and non-waterproof cameras locked in your safe in your stateroom if you've booked a water based tour. On some tours I've had to leave everything in the van. At The Blue Hole we left everything in a pile steps from the road. On one visit part of the trail was washed out and we had to wade through the water to see the upper falls. We had no choice but to leave everything behind. For your own peace of mind, leave your valuables on board.

Just steps from where the taxi dropped us off was a beautiful swimming hole. We were in the middle of the jungle. Everything looked and felt so natural. Pristine, really. There was a gorgeous waterfall with a rope hanging over it. One of our guides grabbed the rope, swung out over the water, and jumped in. And the line began to form. We were taking turns flying through the air and landing in the blue abyss. When we weren't swinging we were swimming below the waterfall and posing for photos. We did some exploring above the waterfall and even found a natural spa tub; the stream that feeds the waterfall has eroded away a pocket that is just large enough for one person to sit in. The water flowing over my back felt amazing.

We were having so much fun that I assumed this was it. This must be The Blue Hole. But then we started hiking through the jungle. Soon we were at a much, much larger Blue Hole with a much, much larger waterfall. There was no rope swing here, but instead the guides walked me part way down the waterfall. I was supposed to run a few steps and jump. I was terrified the entire time. Walking down a waterfall with water rushing beneath my feet was not a calming experience for me. I had a death grip on my guide's hand and kept yelling for him to slow down. It was not my finest moment, but I was so afraid I was going to slip. When we finally got to the midway point I didn't run, I just jumped. The problem with not running a few steps is the possibility of not clearing the rocks at the bottom. Thankfully I did okay. I got a small cut on the top of my foot, but the scar still brings a smile to my face when I think about how great that day was and how I faced my fears by jumping off the waterfall. In fact, I was so afraid of it that I didn't jump during my first trip. I remember my friends running down the waterfall and jumping off without the guides' assistance. Some of my other friends jumped off a 30-40 foot cliff. I still didn't try those. I'm brave, not stupid.

This larger Blue Hole also has a walk/swim through cave under the waterfall. We walked through the cascading water and crawled along until we emerged through a tiny crevice a bit further up. This gets really tricky with lots of people since parts of the cave are only large enough for one person to fit through at a time.

Take some time to explore above the large waterfall. We followed the water upstream and found smaller waterfalls and more awesome picture spots. It was also much quieter up there while everyone else was still swimming down below.

The best part of The Blue Hole is that there's something for every level of bravery. If you just want to swim or watch, that's fine. Or you can give the rope swing a try. Or you can jump off a cliff. Stay in your comfort zone or challenge yourself. It's up to you. Either way you will create a day you will never forget in perhaps the most beautiful place you will ever see.

SHOPPING

I'm much more familiar with the Falmouth shopping area than I am the shops in Ocho Rios. All of the Falmouth shopping is in the pier area immediately off the ship. It's all very new and very nice. You'll find many of the Caribbean's standard stores such as Diamonds International.

The Falmouth port also has a local crafts market if you're looking for some unique or authentic souvenirs.

DINING

Dairy Queen, Quiznos, and Nathan's Hot Dogs - This trio of familiar brands located in the Falmouth port are just like the ones you know at home. Except way more expensive.

Margaritaville - Also located at the port in Falmouth, Margaritaville has good food and a fun atmosphere. It's a tad expensive, the service was slow, and the music was way too loud (and I was young then!). They had only been open a few weeks at the time of my visit, so hopefully things have improved.

Patties - One of my favorite places is the Jamaican patty cart in the port area in Falmouth. It's a simple lunch, but I love these meat filled pastries. Wash it down with a locally made, grapefruit flavored soda called Ting.

PERFECT DAY

My perfect day in Jamaica would be spent with friends exploring The Blue Hole. However, as a guest I would probably choose the safest route and book a tour through the ship. Check out the tours with Chukka for a wide variety of options; each with differing time commitments and level of activity. Make sure you stop by the Jamaican patty stand for a cheap lunch if you are docked in Falmouth!

BELOW DECK: HOME SWEET HOME

I wasn't sure what to expect in my first cabin. I had been told I would have my own room, but I was expecting something tiny. As a child I toured a submarine that had all the storage under the mattress and one sailor's bed was right next to a torpedo. I was pleasantly surprised when I was shown my new room.

I had a larger closet than I had at home, several drawers, and four large shelves. I actually couldn't imagine anyone bringing enough items on board to fill all of these spaces. This place was massive. Plus I had a double bed that I easily converted to a couch/twin bed to make more floor space. Also, no torpedo.

The bathroom was smaller than I had imagined. I used to joke that you could do everything from the toilet. On one side was the sink to brush your teeth and on the other side was the shower. The whole floor was plastic and contained a drain. I used to clean my bathroom by spraying every surface with the detachable showerhead.

I had a really nice cabin like this on a few ships, but it varied ship to ship. On one ship I had a standard two-person room complete with bunk beds and two closets. It was smaller than my old single room and I'm glad I didn't have to share that space with a stranger. On my last ship I had a smaller single room but it had an extra bed that folded up against the wall which came in handy when my sister cruised with me.

I was then moved into what is called a "single share" cabin. I had my own bedroom, but I shared a bathroom with another crew member. The bathroom was in between our two rooms and contained only a toilet and a shower. This space was less than a foot wider than the toilet. Our separate rooms contained a sink, tiny closet, a few shelves, and a desk that ran the length of the room. Above the desk was my bed which could be folded up, against the wall. At night I would fold my bed down and climb up on my desk chair to get into bed. The entire cabin was only slightly longer than an average twin bed and so narrow that I could not fully extend my arms. The bathroom of my current condo is larger than my final cruise ship living space.

I was never fortunate enough to have a window, called a port-hole, although some crew members have them. Most crew members live on Deck 1 or below, but a few live on the same deck as the Navigational Bridge. No crew members have balconies, not even the Captain. High ranking officers have larger cabins including separate bedrooms and sitting areas.

A couple things I miss about my cabin are the metal walls and the mini-fridge. The metal walls were great because I could hang every-thing with magnets. Artwork, photos, reminders, coat hooks; every-thing was hung with a magnet. The mini-fridge was great because in most cabins it was within reach of the bed. I wasn't a coffee drinker but I did like a Diet Mountain Dew or Diet Coke first thing in the morn-ing and on the ship I could have one without even getting out of bed.

DOMINICAN REPUBLIC

A day in Samana, Dominican Republic is another perfect time to book a tour. First of all it is a tender port, meaning there is no dock. Ships anchor offshore and guests board smaller boats to be taken to town. Plan ahead. The tenders won't leave the ship as soon as you board. They'll leave when they're full or when another tender is there to take their place.

> BONUS ADVICE: When tendering, steer clear of peak times to avoid lines and get to shore or back to the ship quickly. For example, it's better to be on the first tender at 7:00 or 8:00. The busy times are 9:00 to 11:00 and you may encounter a wait. Similarly, plan to get back a couple hours early. Maybe book a spa treatment, spend some time at the pool, or enjoy a pre-dinner nap. Excursions frequently include a private tender to shore.

A tour is also a great option for Samana because there isn't much happening downtown. Not much to see or do. Not many places to shop or eat. But don't judge the Dominican Republic by this town. Book a tour that will get you out and exploring and you will be stunned by the beauty of this country.

I highly recommend that you book a tour through your ship for this port. The added challenge of tendering quickly complicates the situation. When you're on a tour through the ship, the ship's staff knows where you are and the ship will wait for you if your group is late. Plus, many tour groups will meet on board and you'll all go ashore together to begin your tour. The extra money is worth it here. Book through the ship.

The first tour I took in Samana was an ATV excursion. Everyone in our group had their own ATV and our guide took us down local roads and through neighborhoods. We passed farms and private homes. Kids ran out to the road to wave at us.

One of our first stops included a hike to a waterfall. Early in the hike we had to cross a small stream. There was no bridge, but we walked across sandbags that acted as stepping stones. Local kids were there and they grabbed our hands to help us across. I didn't ask for or need help, but they grabbed my hand. In my naiveté, I viewed this as local hospitality. In reality, the boy didn't leave my side until I tipped him. It felt a bit like extortion; our guide took us to this place where people were waiting for us. They provided a service I didn't want and then asked for money. I informed the ship's staff of this when I returned. If anything happens on one of your ship arranged tours that you are not comfortable with, please inform the ship's staff. They strive to provide positive and memorable experiences for you during your cruise and they want to know if something missed the mark.

> BONUS ADVICE: Carry small bills with you on your tours. There will be many tipping opportunities. Come prepared. Your tour may also include a stop at a local craft or fruit market that you hadn't been expecting. Most of these places won't accept credit cards so having some cash on hand may get you a souvenir or a snack.

Despite the unexpected assistance, the waterfall area was beautiful and a great photo op. The next stop was a beautiful, deserted beach. The water wasn't calm enough for a swim break, but it was a gorgeous area.

The beginning of the year is a surprisingly great time to go whale watching in Samana. When I think whale-watching cruises I think of New England or Alaska, not the Caribbean. But just like your snowbird neighbors who spend the winter in Florida, the humpback whales seen on the summer and fall cruises in New England winter in the Dominican Republic. January through March is mating, as well as birthing, season. The whales are active and if you're lucky you may even spot a baby.

The whale watching tour I took was on a boat about the size of the tender boat. I've seen multi-decked boats for whale watching in those other destinations, but for here it was a small, open air boat. The benefit of this is that you're with a small group. Everyone knows where to look and you are always close to the action and have a good view. The downside is that the open water can get pretty rough and the small boat can get tossed around in the waves. Since it is open air, the wind can also bring the boat's engine fumes back on to you. I have never gotten seasick. I've obviously spent a lot of time on the water. I've spent weeks in the rough waters of the North Atlantic Ocean and I've even done a couple transatlantic sailings, but I've never been closer to being seasick than I was on my whale watching tour. If you're prone to motion sickness, consider whether this is the tour for you.

If you can handle it, you are in for a treat. One huge benefit to whale watching in the Caribbean is the crystal clear waters. You won't just see whales breaching, you will see them swimming below the surface. Since the guides can see them before they surface they are able to tell you where to look and spot whales that otherwise may have gone undetected. You have a great chance of seeing lots of whales.

If you're cruising to Samana in the first few months of the year and decide to not take the whale-watching cruise, spend some time on your balcony or an outer deck. You just might see the ultimate goodbye wave in the form of a breaching humpback whale.

The best tour I took in Samana was to Cayo Levantado. I booked a tour there for my parents and myself during their first cruise. Samana was my least favorite port on their itinerary and perhaps the in the Caribbean, but after their experience at Cayo Levantado it is their favorite port. In fact, when I told my mom I was writing about it today she said, "Mmmmm...paradise."

Cayo Levantado is a small, resort island off the coast of Samana. It is home to a hotel, beautiful beaches, and all kinds of activities. Half of the island is reserved for hotel guests, but the other half is open to public tours. Our tour package included round trip transportation, beach chairs, snorkel gear, floats, and kayak equipment.

After a few hours laying on the beach, basking in the sun, and taking in the gorgeous landscapes, it was time for a swim and snorkel session. I found Cayo Levantado to be the starfish capital of the Caribbean. I had never seen so many starfish in one place, and I haven't since. Many areas immediately offshore are sandy, but a brief swim had us over coral reefs and seeing a wide variety of sea life including an eel.

The rest of our day was spent in the local craft market, in kayaks, laying on the beach, or getting a snack from the island's restaurant. Many cruise ship guests spend the day at Cayo Levantado, but it never felt overly crowded. Book the earliest possible boat there if you want the island to yourself for a bit. Leave extra time to get back to the ship. A large line will form at the dock in the hours immediately prior to All On Board. There is no place to sit while holding your spot in line so this could have you standing in the hot sun for over an hour. Leave a bit earlier and relax onboard. This will give you extra time to find a good whale watching spot for sail out.

SHOPPING

The town of Samana has a few little souvenir shops, but not the jewelry stores you have grown accustomed to seeing. Cayo Levantado has a small crafts market. This is not a shopping port. Spend money on a tour instead.

DINING

I had lunch out in downtown Samana once. It was not spectacular. Again, book a tour here. Many full day tours will have lunch available for purchase and some even have lunch included.

PERFECT DAY

You really can't go wrong with Cayo Levantado. I'm not even a huge beach fan, and I recognize how great it is. I'd jump on the earliest boat there and spend the day sunning, swimming, and snorkeling. Head back in the early afternoon before the rush hits and find a quiet outer deck or get comfortable on the balcony to watch for whales as the sun sets and the ship sails away from the Dominican Republic.

BELOW DECK: THE DAILY BUFFET

"Did you eat the same food as the guests?" is the question I am asked most about my time at sea. My answer typically is, "Yes, but usually a day later. We got the leftovers." I'm not 100% sure if that's accurate, but it seemed like menu items from the dining room would show up in the mess a day later. Sometimes I know that they were the same items on the same day. For example, I could count on tortilla soup on the first night of every cruise.

The first thing to know about food for the crew is that there are often two separate dining rooms or messes. They are typically called the Staff Mess and the Crew Mess. Both feature buffets, but the Staff Mess serves European or American dishes while the Crew Mess often serves dishes from other cultures; such as Indian, Filipino, or Caribbean cuisine. Cruise ships are a cornucopia of ethnicities so this was a blessing for us all. Just as I would not want to eat unfamiliar food for seven months, neither did my fellow crew members from other countries. This way we all got a little taste of home.

On one ship the Staff and Crew Messes were side by side and a friend came and sat down across from me with french fries on his plate. "French fries," I said, "Where were those?" "In the Crew Mess next to the fish heads," he replied. I laughed and got up to go get some fries. When I got over there I noticed he wasn't joking; there were the fish heads right next to the fries. While that would have been an unconventional lunch for me, it was a taste of home for some of my shipmates.

Food for the crew is very redundant. Tortilla soup on the first night is great for the first month or two, but tortilla soup every week six months later isn't as appetizing. Menus for the dining room are repeated cruise after cruise. Why should other ingredients need to be ordered or chefs need to learn new dishes? The crew could typically tell which day of the cruise it was just by looking at the food.

There were some nice surprises though. I worked with one Hotel Director who used to be a chef and liked hosting "Sandwich Day" in the mess. He had a variety of toppings and would custom build our sandwiches on the spot. Most ships would have Ice Cream Day once a month or so. Hand dipped ice cream was standard for guests, but it was a rare and exciting treat for the crew. I used to joke with my friends about how sad it was that we got so excited over these specialty days. Who knew sandwiches and ice cream could bring so much joy?

Every ship I was on tried to offer a variety for each meal. If I didn't like the entrée items there were typically a variety of breads and cheeses, cereal, and a few ships even had grilled chicken breast each night. I wasn't always eating what I would have chosen for myself, but I never went hungry.

SAN JUAN

The sail in and sail out of San Juan are not to be missed! Which one you catch will depend on the time of day your ship calls on San Juan. My first ship arrived in the late afternoon and left around midnight. Another ship arrived before dawn and left in the late afternoon. Check your ship's itinerary and plan to be on an upper, outer deck as you arrive or depart. You will sail right past Castillo San Felipe del Morro; a fort on the corner of Old San Juan. You can also see Castillo de San Cristóbal down the coast.

If your ship docks in Old San Juan you are steps from restaurants, sights, and shopping. If you dock at the Pan American Pier, you are a short cab ride from the heart of downtown Old San Juan.

If you have an American cell phone service provider, your phone will probably work in San Juan with no extra fees. Check with your provider before your trip to confirm.

It rained during most of my calls on San Juan. Oftentimes it was just a brief shower. It's a good idea to take an umbrella out with you or purchase one from a shop downtown if you don't want to pack it. The umbrella I still use today was bought at the Marshalls in Old San Juan one rainy night.

While it is possible to visit a beach or do a beach excursion in San Juan, you will likely have much more convenient beaches in other ports of call during your cruise. Consider saving the beach trip for later.

If you are able, I recommend doing a walking tour of Old San Juan. Your ship will probably offer a guided tour or you can do some preliminary research and put together a self-guided tour. If you are docked at the Old San Juan pier, turn left at the end of the pier and follow the water. You will walk through Dársenas Square and see the United States Coast Guard boats to your left. Many of the streets in this part of town look like blue cobblestone. They are actually cobalt bricks, which were used as ballast in early ships arriving to San Juan.

I recommend continuing on to Paseo de la Princesa and walking down the tree-lined alley until you reach a fountain. The fountain with the open water behind it makes a great photo op, but don't stand too close — many tourists get sprayed when winds from the open ocean make their way down the channel and force the fountain's water out of its intended path.

Just past the fountain there is a path to the right. This path follows the water outside the city's walls. You will walk below La Fortaleza, the residence of the Governor of San Juan. I always enjoyed this walk along the water. It is slower and quieter than downtown. I would frequently see locals fishing from the pier, children playing, and couples walking. For me, it was a way to absorb my surroundings.

You will soon reach the red City Gate. The original Port of San Juan was here and everyone entering the island passed through this gate and up the street to the San Juan Cathedral to thank God for granting them a safe trip. The path along the water continues on and becomes the Paseo del Morro. The first time I took the path past the City Gate I assumed that it went all the way to Castillo San Felipe del Morro. While the path parallels the walls of the fort, at the time I walked it, there was no way through. It was just a nice walk and a dead end. According to the National Park Service, there are future plans to add an entrance to the fort.

If you continue along the water or turn up through the City Gate, I can guarantee you one sight: stray cats. I have no idea why they are there, but I saw cats on every single trip.

I also recommend checking out the two forts you saw as you were sailing into San Juan: Castillo San Felipe del Morro and Castillo de San Cristóbal. Both sites are managed by the National Park Service and require an entrance fee. They offer beautiful views along with educational opportunities. If you are a history buff or traveling with kids, this stop is a must. Take a family photo with a cannon or squeeze everyone into a sentry box.

On nice days the lawn of San Felipe will be covered with families flying kites. Plan ahead and pack a cheap kite for your trip. If you're unprepared but decide to join in, there are often street vendors nearby selling kites. I was on a ship with the home port of San Juan for a few months. I bought a cheap kite and took it out as often as I could.

I found the time on the lawn freeing and a chance to blend into local life.

For the more adventurous, stop by the cemetery between the two forts. The back wall is built on the coastline and there used to be a crack in the wall you could slip through and do some exploring along the shore. Great views, but a hazardous location. If the crack is still there, pass through it at your own risk.

SHOPPING

The architecture won't fool you. You'll know you are in America. Old Town San Juan has US favorites such as Marshalls, CVS, and Walgreens. A quick cab ride can take you to Plaza las Americas where you'll find all the comforts of home in Macy's, Victoria's Secret, Forever 21, and many more stores. If you realize you forgot to pack something or have run out of an essential, San Juan is a great place to restock.

San Juan has many of the big jewelry stores the Caribbean is known for: Diamonds International, EFFY Jewelers, Colombian Emeralds, etc. However, I've been told that the prices and selection are better in St. Thomas. But remember the first rule of shopping, "If you see it and you like it, buy it." What you find in stock here may not be in stock on the next island. So buy a piece if you fall in love with it.

Old Town San Juan offers many discount souvenir shops with picture frames, beach towels, t-shirts, and other items to materially immortalize your cruise.

DINING

Blizz. Yogurt - In my cruising days, yogurt parlors were a new concept. A few years later they are now ubiquitous. However, Blizz was always a much anticipated treat in the San Juan heat. It's just down the street from San Cristobal on the corner of San Francisco and Norzagaray streets. Choose your flavor and toppings then enjoy in the air conditioning! Blizz was rarely crowded and had fast wifi. A great place to cool off and take a break.

Brickhaus - I had heard Brickhaus was known for their wings. I went there for my birthday one year and was unimpressed. This sports bar is a tiny venue that sometimes hosts live music. The volume is too much for the dinner crowd, but great for those looking to party.

Pizza e Birra - I visited San Juan a couple times a month for a couple years. Sadly, it was at the end of my time there that I discovered Pizza e Birra. It is in the courtyard of the El Convento hotel, just up the street from the City Gate, and is home to some of the best pizza I ever had (and that includes during my contract that took me to Italy). You may not instantly think "pizza" when you think Puerto Rican food, but this place is incredible!

> BONUS ADVICE: No cooked food can be brought back onboard. Even if you just had the most amazing meal, don't buy another one and bring it with you. To this day, I still have it in my mind that I cannot take food back to my office. Really. It happened this week. You are clear to bring back packaged food. So buy all the souvenir taffy and chocolate you can carry.

Starbucks - Cell phone service and Starbucks. It's easy to see that Puerto Rico is a US territory. If you're a Starbucks addict make sure you stop here for a rare fix. This is one of the few Caribbean locations of this beloved chain.

PERFECT DAY

I would begin by watching the ship sail into port. Disembark and walk along the water and through the City Gate. Stop for a delicious meal at Pizza e Birra before heading to the forts. While I recommend touring Castillo San Felipe del Morro and Castillo de San Cristóbal, if you've toured them in the past I recommend buying a kite and feeling like a kid again while spending time on the lawn. After a day in the sun you'll be ready to cool down with some yogurt at Blizz. And of course, use that cell phone to check in on everyone at home.

BELOW DECK: CONTRACT LENGTH

Before joining my first ship I was told my contract length would be six and a half months. My shortest contract was six months and ten days. My longest contract was around nine months. But on average they were around six and a half months. That's a fairly common average for people in entertainment like me. A lot of the performers, technicians, and activity staff are there for that amount of time. Many of the managers worked four-month contracts.

During our contracts we work every single day. There's no such thing as a day off. Cruise ships are a 24/7 enterprise. Have you ever heard of a hotel closing down on the weekends? No. When one guest leaves, they prepare for the arrival of the next. That's how it is on ships too. One round of guests leave in the morning and a few hours later we're sailing away from port with brand new guests.

At the end of my contract I typically had two months off. I would spend the first few weeks sleeping, watching television, seeing my family, and eating all of my favorite foods I hadn't tasted in a while. After I was rested, I really had a lot to pack into my remaining time. I would travel to visit friends or attend a conference; I even took a weeklong certification course during one vacation.

Being on the ship was great, but having two solid months of free time to spend with the people I loved was better. I missed weddings, birthdays, and every holiday imaginable by being at sea for nearly seven months at a time. So it was great to take my time off to spend with everyone I loved.

ST. THOMAS

Chances are good that your Caribbean cruise itinerary will include a stop in St. Thomas. This island offers a great mix of shopping, dining, beaches, and adventure.

Ships dock in either Havensight or Crown Bay. Both are close to downtown Charlotte Amalie, the capital of the United States Virgin Islands. Crown Bay is a newer cruise port so shops and restaurants are beginning to pop up along the pier, but it is not as well established as Havensight, which offers an entire mall with many shops and restaurants right at the end of the gangway.

Getting around the island is easy. Open air taxis are ubiquitous and will take you wherever you want to go. Your Port and Shopping Guide on board should be able to tell you how much a ride will cost you from the ship to downtown. It's usually around $4.00. Outside the ship, in the taxi line, you will often find people going to the same place you are or people just looking to go to a beach. The open air taxis fit about 12-16 people and the driver will want to take as many as possible, so be prepared to wait a few minutes as the seats fill up. Keep this in mind when you're planning what time to return to the ship. Don't cut it too close to All On Board time as your taxi driver may try to wait for more fares. Also, the roads get congested in the last hour before All On Board. Plan to get back a bit earlier and explore the port area to use your time most efficiently.

St. Thomas is known for its beautiful beaches, but none are in sight when immediately off the ship. Magens Bay is one of the most popular and is said to be one of the most beautiful beaches in the world. If your ship docks in Crown Bay, I highly recommend you check out Emerald Bay. I discovered Emerald Bay late in my cruise ship career, but it quickly became one of my favorite spots. I was suspicious on my first visit when my taxi dropped me off in the parking lot of a Best Western, but after I walked through the lobby, I was greeted by a pool, gorgeous beach, and a bar and restaurant. My friends and I typically started our day laying on the beach before enjoying free wifi over lunch in the restaurant and swimming in the pool throughout the afternoon. There are a couple iguanas that frequent the pool, so keep a watchful eye for a chance to make a new friend. If you paid attention on the drive over, you can easily walk back to the ship.

On my last trip to St. Thomas I went to Emerald Bay and tried flyboarding with St. Thomas Flyboard. I was terrible! But the staff was helpful and friendly. They even let my friend ride out on the jet ski with my instructor so he could film my failure. Even though I've now confirmed that I have no future in flyboarding, I'm glad I gave it a try and saw the island from a new perspective. After all, cruising should be about trying new things.

I also recommend Coki Beach. Coki is further away, but is still a less than 30 minute cab ride. Coki Beach is alongside Coral World Ocean Park. The water here has a sandy bottom and many small fish near the rocks. One fish I can almost guarantee you will see is a sergeant major. You can rent snorkel gear from a nearby Coral World hut.

> BONUS ADVICE: If you already know how to snorkel and plan on visiting more than one beach on your cruise vacation, I recommend buying your own mask and snorkel. You can find a set for $25.00 or less in the souvenir shops on the islands. Now you'll be prepared to snorkel anywhere your adventures take you. If you've never snorkeled before, consider booking a snorkeling excursion through your ship. Instruction is provided and the gear is supplied. It's a great way to literally get your feet wet and decide if snorkeling is a hobby for you.

Coral World charges an entrance fee and will bring you face to face with sea creatures through exhibits such as the Turtle Pool, Caribbean Reef Encounter, Stingray Lagoon, and Touch Pool. They also have an Undersea Observation Tower - like a lookout tower - except under the surface of the ocean. To get even closer to the animals, you can book additional experiences that will have you swimming with turtles, sea lions, and sharks. Coral World also offers rides on a Nautilus Semi Submarine. In this semi-submersible vehicle each passenger has his or her own window to see underwater as they sail along. What you see is all up to nature and what decides to swim past the windows. I took this semi-sub ride on my first Christmas

Eve away from home. Part way through my ride, a diver entered the water and fed the fish, bringing them right to my window. It's a Christmas I will never forget.

Another one of my favorite tours was a kayak and snorkel tour of Cas Cay. It was offered through the ship and was facilitated by Virgin Island Eco Tours. The tour began with brief kayaking instruction before setting out through the mangrove forest. At the time, mangroves were new to me so I really enjoyed learning about the benefits of mangroves and their ecosystems. For example, small fish (even baby sharks) stay in mangrove forests because predators can't get into the small spaces created by the root structure.

Once we arrived at Cas Cay, we took a brief hike, learned about the ecosystem, and had a hermit crab race with local hermit crabs that we found on the island. We then hiked out to a blowhole where we created beautiful photographs with the risk of getting drenched. The tour included time to snorkel complete with snorkeling instruction. We saw multiple species of fish and a sunken boat. Even if you are an inexperienced kayaker or snorkeler, this is a great tour for active cruisers ready to work off some of the buffet.

If your ship is docked in Havensight, Paradise Point is a must! This enclosed skyride whisks you up Flag Hill for a jaw dropping view of Charlotte Amalie. At the top, enjoy breathtaking scenery, countless photo ops, unique shops, a restaurant, and even an exotic bird show. If this is your first trip the Caribbean, you will be amazed at the clear blue waters stretching as far as the eye can see. On a clear day you can see all the way to Puerto Rico. The Skyride to Paradise Point begins such a short walk from the pier that you have no excuse to not go check it out.

BONUS ADVICE: Carry cash! On my parents' first cruise we spent the day shopping downtown. We had lots of time before All On Board so we decided to check out the Skyride to Paradise Point. We all had credit cards, but little cash, and the credit card machine was out of service. I left my parents to wander around Havensight Mall as I sprinted back to the ship, grabbed a handful of cash, and dashed back outside to find them again. It all worked out and we loved our time at Paradise Point and still display pictures from that day in our homes. However, if we hadn't been so close to the ship we may have missed out or at least greatly cut short our time to explore. Come prepared for anything.

No matter which pier your ship docks at, consider walking to town. Taxis will have you downtown in about 10 to 15 minutes. Walking takes two or three times longer, but you get to see and enjoy more of the island.

The walk from Crown Bay to downtown is about 35 minutes. You'll first walk through the Crown Bay marina and gaze at several yachts. The next 15 minutes of the journey always felt and looked a little sketchy, but I never had any problems. I viewed this walk past stores, schools, and a post office as a look at real life on St. Thomas instead of just the polished tourist spots I was expected to see. You'll soon pass a seaplane dock where I frequently saw planes taking off or landing. The rest of the walk will be along the water. Enjoy the view of islands in the distance and clear water. The water is so clear that I often saw fish swimming offshore.

If you are docked in Havensight, a quick trip through Havensight Mall will have you in Yacht Haven Grande. The yachts that call this place home will make you drool in jealousy. I frequently saw a yacht docked here with a helicopter on board. A helicopter! Yacht Haven Grande is home to several shops and restaurants. The brick walkways will lead you past fountains and oftentimes iguanas. It connects to a paved sidewalk that will have you downtown in about 15 minutes. Again, the water is so clear that I frequently saw fish along my journey.

If you plan on spending time downtown, consider taking a break from shopping to climb the 99 Steps to Blackbeard's Castle. Count as you go along and see if the name is correct. At the top there is an entrance fee to the Castle, but you'll enjoy yet another panoramic view of St. Thomas. Explore the grounds, learn about pirate history and legends, climb the tower, and pose for pictures with pirate statues. Your entrance fee also includes access to the pool and entrance to several other nearby sites such as restored homes originally built in the 1800s and a two story Amber Waterfall made of around 12,000 pieces of amber. Blackbeard's Castle is an often overlooked St. Thomas gem. It's slightly off the beaten path, but offers a variety of activities making this a great stop for families.

If you've shopped until you dropped from the Caribbean heat, cool off in Magic Ice. This ice gallery is complete with numerous ice sculptures, ice structures, an ice slide you can ride, and an ice bar at which you can order perfectly chilled drinks. The friendly staff at Magic Ice will furnish you with a parka, gloves, and leggings so you can linger in the majestic, man-made winter wonderland. It's a great place to spend an hour and get refreshed.

If you've been to St. Thomas several times and you feel like you've seen and done it all, don't just sit onboard all day. Consider taking a ferry to St. John, USVI. Your ship will probably offer excursions to St. John, but you can also take a ferry there on your own. Ferries depart from Charlotte Amalie and Red Hook (a taxi ride away). Obviously this trip is best done when you have an extended time in port. Be very mindful of the time as missing your ferry could mean missing your ship. But the beauty of St. John is worth the effort. I cover what to see and do in St. John in the next chapter.

SHOPPING

St. Thomas is well known for its abundance of shopping opportunities and great deals. Shopping on St. Thomas is duty free so you will often find items much cheaper than you would at home. Like I said before, it's a good idea to know what you're looking for and what you're willing to pay as you may experience a high amount of sales pressure in some of these stores. Check with your ship's staff, specifically your onboard Shopping Guide, for current customs information.

A few of the major shops St. Thomas is known for are Diamonds International, Tanzanite International, and EFFY Jewelers. But there are many, many more. Novelty shops include Del Sol, where everything changes color in the sun, and Cariloha, a bamboo product retailer. Stop in Mr. Tablecloth for great gifts or practical souvenirs. You can also find discount electronics at Royal Caribbean (not to be confused with the cruise line).

BONUS ADVICE: I purchased an underwater digital camera from Royal Caribbean. I not only got a great deal, but it was probably the best purchase I ever made for life on a cruise ship. If you haven't bought one before your cruise, consider buying one in your first port. Many waterproof cameras are also freezeproof and shock-proof. They are great for snorkeling and river tubing trips as well as taking pictures in the rain without risking damage to your more expensive camera. Because of the camera's rugged exterior and shockproof quality, I used to clip mine to the waistbelt on my backpack while I was hiking. My camera has bounced off rocks on trails, been dropped numerous times, and still works great. If you plan on spending time in or under the water on your cruise, consider making this investment to capture those memories.

Both Havensight and Crown Bay have smaller shopping areas. Yacht Haven Grande has additional shopping opportunities. But if you're serious about shopping, you need to go downtown. Traveling the few extra minutes into the heart of Charlotte Amalie will get you a better selection and possibly even bigger discounts.

DINING

HAVENSIGHT

Hooters - I came here once or twice for wings. It's exactly as you would expect. Same food and atmosphere as in the US.

Pizza Amore - It's by no means the best pizza in the Caribbean, but it is a good, quick, cheap bite. If going on a cruise hasn't made you feel like a kid again, walking in here will. The interior is decorated with old metal signs and feels like a step back in time. There is limited seating so you may need to take the party outside. The slices are huge. Don't overestimate how hungry you are as you cannot bring your leftovers back onboard (and with the buffet that awaits you, why would you want to?!?).

Pizza Amore is located just outside Havensight Mall, across French-man's Bay Road. They didn't have wifi during most of my visits, but on my last trip there they finally had it! Surf, eat, and relax!

Shipwreck - Best Burger on the Island! Or so the sign inside says. This delightful pub is in the same building as Pizza Amore, but at the opposite end. If the sign doesn't catch your attention, perhaps the life-size shark model will. This is a fun sports bar with cozy booths, multiple screens, wifi, and outdoor seating.

My go-to Shipwreck order was the three-quarter pound burger. I tried most of the burgers on their menu, but my favorite was a modified Buffalo Burger, with bacon and cheddar instead of blue cheese. My mouth is watering as I write this!

I first started going to Shipwreck when I was on a ship that docked in Havensight. I ended my sailing career on a ship that docked in Crown Bay and nearly every St. Thomas visit I would walk an hour across Charlotte Amalie to get lunch here. It's that good! The burger and seasoned fries were so enormous, I oftentimes wouldn't eat din-ner that night.

The quality of Shipwreck's food began to go down on my last few vis-its, but I'm hoping they were just in a slump. I guarantee you that if I ever get to go back to St. Thomas again, you'll find me at Shipwreck.

YACHT HAVEN

Bad Ass Coffee - I'm not much of a coffee drinker and a hot beverage was the last thing I wanted in the Caribbean, but Bad Ass really grew on me. There is wifi and extremely limited seating. They have one television and it's usually playing news - sometimes this was a rude awakening from the fantasy land that cruising can become.

Aside from brewed coffees, Bad Ass offers smoothies, blended cof-fee drinks, and a variety of pastries. Located in Yacht Haven Grande, Bad Ass Coffee is a great way to start your morning on your way into town or a fantastic pit stop to check your email and get a cool drink on your way back if your ship is docked in Havensight.

Grande Cru - I may have only eaten here once, but the kobe beef burger was amazing. This place is obviously not as affordable as

Shipwreck, but if you're looking for a splurge, this is a good place to do it. The open air seating places you on a pier overlooking the marina at Yacht Haven Grande. If you can tear your gaze from the yachts for a moment, look in to the shallow, clear water next to you. You will easily be able to spot several species of fish. Grande Cru has the best dining atmosphere of anywhere I've eaten on the island.

DOWNTOWN

Pizza Hut - It's right next door to Magic Ice. The food is the same you're familiar with, but be prepared to pay a bit more. Get it to go and cross the street to eat next to the water.

ELSEWHERE

Duffy's Love Shack - Duffy's serves up drinks and souvenirs in one! Each drink comes in a themed glass you can take home with you. On my first visit I had the "Zoom, Zoom Shooter." It was a shot glass glued to the top of a pull back racer with a slide whistle as a stir stick. I had to do something along the lines of: do the shot, shout my own name, spin around three times, pull back the car, and blow the whistle. I was racing a colleague of mine. I don't remember who won. I think that's the point.

On that trip a couple of my friends got the "Shark Tank." It is a fish bowl full of rum. Really! If you're looking to try some of the Caribbean's rum, order the Shark Tank and sample six kinds all at once. You'll also find little trinkets like toy sharks floating the clear blue "water" - as if this drink needed anything to make it better.

I still have my "Zoom, Zoom Shooter" shot glass along with my mini tiki shot glass from another trip when I tried "Gods R Crazy." That one tasted like candy! Dangerous stuff. Along with my shot glasses I have a couple of the plastic leis they gave us and a sticker announcing to the world that "I got lei'd at Duffy's Love Shack."

Duffy's is an atypical bar in an atypical location. It's in a parking lot of a strip mall and it's not really next to any big tourist destinations. You can easily go here after a day at Coki Beach or after a tour with Virgin Island EcoTours. You could also make a special trip. Duffy's is about a 15 minute cab ride from the Havensight pier and still less than half an hour from Crown Bay. Due to the semi-inconvenient location, be sure to give your taxi driver a time to return for you. Hailing a taxi in this part of the island is a bit more difficult than it is elsewhere.

PERFECT DAY

This is a tough one. St. Thomas has so many great options. But here are a couple sample itineraries:

Havensight Docked Ship - Get off the ship and walk through Yacht Haven Grande and do some shopping downtown. Return to Havensight in time for lunch at Shipwreck. Then head over to the Skyride to Paradise Point and take in the views. If you're not into shopping, catch an early cab over to Coki Beach. Head back to Havensight before the afternoon sun gets unbearable. Lunch at Shipwreck and Skyride to Paradise Point.

Crown Bay Docked Ship - Get off the ship and walk through Crown Bay Marina for shopping downtown. Catch a cab back but head over to Emerald Bay for the rest of your time. Get lunch, swim in the pool, lay on the sand, or try flyboarding.

BELOW DECK: SHARP DRESSED WOMAN

I might be alone in this thought, but I loved wearing a uniform. I was quite fortunate and had a great uniform. During the day I wore a white polo shirt, khaki shorts or pants, and white shoes. After 6:00 pm I had to change into my evening uniform, which was a white polo, black pants, and black shoes. On formal nights I wore formal attire. If I was going out to dinner or to spend time in one of the guest area bars I needed to dress according to the attire specified for our guests on that night. The mantra of my supervisors was often, "We have to look better than the guests."

No uniform was complete without a nametag. After a while I could tell when I didn't have mine on and I felt incomplete. I also would never leave my cabin or my office without my onboard phone so I could always be reached. I also always carried my Cruise Compass, which contained the activities schedule for the day and other helpful information.

And a smile. We were told we were out of uniform if we weren't wearing a smile.

ST. JOHN

St. John is not actually a cruise port. But as I mentioned in the last chapter, many guests visiting St. Thomas find their way over to St. John. I visited St. John a few times and though I love all of USVI, St. John is the island on the top of my list.

In the last chapter I mentioned the ferry from St. Thomas to St. John. Ferries leave St. Thomas from Charlotte Amalie and Red Hook. Ferries arrive in St. John at Cruz Bay. While it may look similar to other islands upon arrival, beyond Cruz Bay is peace and tranquility not found in most cruise ship destinations. Much of this is due to the fact that the majority of St. John is actually Virgin Islands National Park. Just taking a cab ride around the island is breathtaking. The views from some of the major roads are incredible.

I didn't make it to St. John often enough and I can't wait to go back and explore more. All of the beaches I experienced were stunning. These are some of the best beaches you will find in the Caribbean and they are far less crowded than the beaches in other ports.

My first trip to St. John was on an excursion from the ship and it was a trip to snorkel the underwater trail at Trunk Bay. Before that day I had never heard of an underwater trail. It is similar to historical walks found in almost any city in America. On these walks there is a set path with informational signs regarding nearby buildings or what happened on this location in the past. The sign then provides directions to the next stop. On an underwater trail, you swim and snorkel from sign to sign. Each sign has pictures and information to help you identify different species of fish and coral. This experience will spoil you for all other snorkeling adventures, where you will be seeing so many beautiful things with no way of identifying them. This was one of my first snorkeling experiences and I was hooked. The Caribbean is beautiful and half its beauty is under the surface of the water.

My next trip to St. John took me to Cinnamon Bay. The peace and solitude was unlike anything I had encountered in the Caribbean. This is one gorgeous place of unspoiled property. For once, reality is as good as the website.

SHOPPING

Cruz Bay has a few stores. Plan to get back into town early to alleviate fear of missing the ferry back to St. Thomas. Use the extra time to peruse the shops.

DINING

Trunk Bay - There is a little snack shack here to satisfy your hunger until you get back to the ship.

T'ree Lizards Restaurant - Located at Cinnamon Bay, this restaurant is built around a tree. The atmosphere and the wooden flooring give you the feeling of eating lunch in a tree house. Take a moment to pet the friendly cat that wanders the property.

PERFECT DAY

You're in St. John. Everyday is perfect.

BELOW DECK: LAUNDRY DAY

Just like in real life, laundry day is the worst day on a cruise ship. First off, there are no in-unit washers or dryers. You have two options: 1. You can pay per item to have everything washed or 2. You can gather a few quarters and go do it yourself.

Every ship had a laundry room or two. It was usually covered in lint and if all of the machines hit the spin cycle at the same time the floor would flood. An added little game was trying to pick the machines that would actually work. There were always a few washers that would fill up with water but wouldn't drain and dryers that didn't actually dry. The laundry rooms were rarely in a convenient location. I was never across the hall or around the corner from one. In fact, on my final ship I had to carry my laundry bag up one deck, through the mess (mmm....doesn't that sound nice? People hauling dirty clothes past your food.), and back down two decks.

I usually brought a book and stayed with my laundry the whole time due to the oddities of the machines. Well, that and to avoid other people touching my clothes. If I left my machine unattended and didn't get back the moment the cycle was finished, my clothes might be removed by another crew member. I found my clean clothes on a linty, dirty table mixed in with other people's clothes and even on the floor, the nasty, flooded floor. I once came back and found one of my Sports Staff friends folding my clothes. Even my underwear. Yes, that's better than having it thrown on the floor, but ladies, think about one of your male colleagues folding your underwear. This is probably why an in-unit washer and dryer were such a sticking point for me when I was choosing my first apartment after cruise ships.

ST. CROIX

I thought I had seen and done all USVI had to offer with my trips to St. Thomas and St. John. I was pleasantly surprised by how much more I still had to see when I joined a ship that called on St. Croix.

My ship docked in Frederiksted where, at the end of a long pier, Fort Frederik is located. Fort Frederik is now a museum where I visited exhibits and learned about the past of Frederiksted and St. Croix. It also offered great views of my ship and a chance to take a photograph of a cannon aiming right at my floating home.

St. Croix is also a well-known diving destination. I completed my PADI Open Water Diver certification on the Explorer of the Seas (more on this in the St. Maarten chapter). Check with your cruise line before you sail if you are interested in becoming a certified diver. However, consider getting certified before you go so you're not spending your vacation taking classes and quizzes.

St. Croix diving is famous for The Wall. Coral reefs and their accompanying ecosystems are normally seen from above as they are typically on the ocean floor. However, The Wall is a sheer drop-off covered in coral with fish swimming all around. It offers a unique perspective to the underwater world.

I dove with Cane Bay Dive Shop. Diving to The Wall is an easy shore dive. We simply walked across the street from the dive shop, down the beach, and into the water. A short swim had us at The Wall. While each dive will be different, a couple highlights from mine were a stingray and a carousel horse. No, a carousel horse is not a rare species of fish you have never heard of, it is literally a sunken carousel horse.

St. Croix is also known for its turtles. Not far from the pier in Frederiksted is Sandy Point National Wildlife Refuge. It is only open on Saturdays and Sundays, and my ship called on St. Croix mid-week so I, unfortunately, never got to go. If your ship is in on the weekend, go for it!

There is a nice area of public beaches between the pier at

Frederiksted and Sandy Point. Once you reach the end of the pier, Fort Frederik is on your left, but turn right. Keep walking until you are out of town. The road is called Veteran's Shore Drive. You'll soon see sand and you can now walk along the beach. You'll pass two hotels with beach chairs and umbrellas out for their guests. Go further and find a less busy patch of beach. The swimming here is good and the snorkeling is decent as well. I saw several large schools of fish and at one point I looked over to find a sea turtle swimming beside me. It was a magical experience. I can't even describe how beautiful it was to be swimming along with such a graceful creature.

The one excursion I took from the ship was a snorkel trip to Buck Island. It began with a drive to Christiansted; the other city on St. Croix. From there we boarded a boat for the journey out to Buck Island. The boat moored off the shore and we jumped in the water. Snorkel equipment was provided and instruction was given.

There is an underwater trail similar to the one in Trunk Bay in St. John. However, the signs on this trail were covered in sediment and not easily readable. There were guides on hand to answer questions and point out highlights of the underwater realm. The water here was rougher than on my snorkel trips from shore, but it was easily manageable with the life vest that was provided.

SHOPPING

The only thing I bought in St. Croix was a t-shirt from Cane Bay Dive Shop. Check with your onboard Shopping Guide for more information, but you will find a bigger selection in some of the other islands such as St. Thomas and St. Maarten.

DINING

FREDERIKSTED

Turtles Deli - I found this spot early in my adventures to St. Croix and I returned trip after trip. Turtles Deli is just a small shop with outdoor seating comprised of plastic patio furniture. It is conveniently located in the southern end of Frederiksted and is a perfect pit stop on the way to the beach. They serve up huge sandwiches; enough to fuel a day full of adventure. A couple of my favorites were the Smokin

Chix and the Turkey Reuben. At the time, I was a Diet Mountain Dew addict and this place was the only restaurant I found in the entire Caribbean that served Diet Mountain Dew. I'm not sure if it was the soda, the sandwiches, or the amazing views, but Turtles Deli won my heart and my repeat business.

> BONUS ADVICE: Consider packing your favorite beverage for your cruise. While you're not allowed to bring alcohol onboard (any you purchase in port will be collected at the gangway and distributed to you before departure on the last day), I have seen people bring on cases of bottled water or their favorite soda. Your brand of choice may not be available where you are headed so consider bringing some with you.

Cane Bay

Eat @ Cane Bay - A great, post-dive eatery serving up huge burgers and lots of options. With tons of open air seating, this place is located across from the beach and next to Cane Bay Dive Shop.

PERFECT DAY

If it's your first time in St. Croix, begin your day by checking out Fort Frederik and learning about the area. Wander through town as you make your way to Turtles Deli for lunch. Continue on for an afternoon at the beach complete with snorkeling and hopefully even a turtle sighting.

If you're a certified diver, don't miss the chance to dive The Wall. It's a unique experience not offered in most dive sites. If you're not a diver, but love marine ecosystems, consider booking the Buck Island snorkel excursion. You'll have access to many species while remaining on the surface.

St. Croix is a small island with large possibilities. It offers great learning opportunities, beaches, diving, and food. Enjoy your day! It's impossible not to here.

BELOW DECK: CABIN CLEANING

I lived in such a small space that cleaning was easy, right? Unfortunately, no. First off, I didn't have any cleaning supplies. If you live in one room, you don't buy a vacuum. And all of the environmental regulations restricted which cleaning products we could use. Vacuums and cleaning supplies were available to be "checked out" by signing a sheet or turning over my SeaPass card for the duration of their use. Much like the laundry rooms, these stations were never across the hall or around the corner. It often meant walking across the ship and probably even to another deck, then carrying the supplies up or down the stairs to my cabin where it would take me less than five minutes to thoroughly clean.

Clean sheets and towels were an entirely separate battle. It was great that the ship provided them for me but I was forced with dealing with the laundry situation to wash them myself or going to the Linen Room to get new ones. The Linen Room was located on one of the lowest decks on the ship; anywhere from two to four decks below mine. It was managed by a crew member with the title "Linen Keeper." The Linen Keeper took his (in my experience the Linen Keeper was typically male) job very seriously. I could only get new linens after turning in my old linens, and different sheets and towels were allocated for different ranks. The Linen Keeper was there to manage every aspect of this process. I'm not sure what other duties the Linen Keeper had, but he only opened the Linen Room for the crew a few hours each day.

When we got to the Linen Room we had to present our old linens and request the types and quantities of the new linens we wanted. I wasn't allowed to just get the items off the shelf myself. I had to say what I needed and someone would get it for me. Unfortunately, they didn't always have what I needed and weren't great at communicating that up front. I once walked in with a wet towel and asked for a new one. The Linen Keeper motioned at a bin for my old towel. When I turned back around he said, "We don't have any clean crew towels." Instead of giving me a guest towel, I simply had no towels until I could come back a day later.

Getting toilet paper could be even more of a hassle. The Linen Keeper was also the Toilet Paper Keeper. There were times it was rationed and I'd only be given one roll when I had asked for two. There was a ship where I had to sign and date a sheet before I could take the toilet paper. And forget tissues. I didn't have a high enough rank for a box of tissues.

The easiest way around all of this was to befriend the housekeeping staff along my normal routes. I got to know one of the staff and every so often I would stop and ask for sheets or a roll of toilet paper. On a couple ships we got really lucky and found linen closets that weren't locked at night, which we raided to restock our supplies. It's the little things in life. I hate to admit this, but I even paid for someone else to come clean my cabin and provide new sheets and towels. I lived in a seven foot square cube, but it was easier to pay someone than run around the ship gathering supplies.

ST. MAARTEN

St. Maarten is my favorite island in the Caribbean. Everything is close by and convenient. The scenery is gorgeous and the water is clear. St. Maarten also offers more diversity than most ports as the island is divided into French and Dutch sides.

Most ships dock in Philipsburg on the Dutch side. To get downtown you can take a taxi, a water taxi, or walk. I recommend taking the water taxi or walking. The water taxi pier is in the port area. Just follow the signs. There is usually a small, flat fee that will get you a wristband for unlimited rides throughout the day.

To reach downtown on foot, walk toward the taxi stand and follow the driveway out to the main road. Turn left and follow the sidewalk into town. Look for mountain goats grazing and playing on the large cliff across the street. Along the walk there is sometimes a man with a card table or a cooler selling cold drinks. Stop and buy a bottle of Desperados. Desperados is essentially tequila flavored beer. If you like either of those, you'll love them together. Desperados are mainly found in Europe, but they're slowly making their way across the pond. They can now be found on a few islands and, recently, in Florida. But they are scarce, so enjoy while you can. Plus, in St. Maarten you can walk with your drink, so sip away on your walk to town.

You'll soon be in a parking lot you can cut through to get to the beach. And here is the beauty of St. Maarten: the beach is bordered by a row of restaurants that is bordered by a row of shops. You can easily swim, eat, and shop all in one day!

If you're looking for more than that, there are numerous great excursions available from Philipsburg. I mentioned earlier that I became a PADI certified diver on a cruise ship. Contact the cruise line you are sailing with to see if this is a possibility for you. My class involved coursework in a conference room and a couple dives in the pool onboard. Then, I did my certification dives in St. Maarten. Everything was arranged through the ship, but we dove with Scuba Fun Center. This dive shop is located halfway along the walk into town. We dove at the base of Fort Amsterdam; the dilapidated fort that can be seen across the bay from the cruise ship pier. On the day I got certified the visibility was poor, but my dive instructor was still able to show us a few highlights including a cannon that is believed to have fallen off the fort towering above. Poor visibility is a fairly common problem in St. Maarten, but there's a lot to see if you can get a clear day.

I also set sail with Captain Morgan on Captain Morgan's Sail and Snorkel tour. You can likely book this tour right on board. We met our tour guide on the pier and were escorted to our waiting vessel nearby. Even though I'd been at sea for months, I loved being on this sailboat with the wind in my hair. After we sailed for a while, we circled back and stopped for snorkeling at the base of Fort Amsterdam near where I had done my certification dives. Our captain gave us general directions of where to look for sunken objects and we set out on what felt like an underwater scavenger hunt. The visibility was much better this day and I not only saw the sunken cannon, I also saw fish and a sunken helicopter. After the snorkeling was over, we enjoyed rum punch and sandwiches back on the sailboat. This tour was in the morning and we returned to Philipsburg with the afternoon to do with as we pleased.

One of the most physically demanding tours I took was the America's Cup Yacht Racing 12 Metre Challenge. If you've ever seen America's Cup or are interested in sailing, this is a great chance to try it out. While you do have an option to just relax on the boat, the idea is that you get to participate in the race. You'll be given a job to do and instructions on how to do it. If there are enough people in your tour group, you will be split into two teams and race each other. Just about everyone in my group was expecting something more relaxing; along the lines of what we experienced with Captain Morgan. However, there were a handful of us ready to race. In the end, we were terrible. We were easily, and soundly, defeated.

BONUS ADVICE: A tour that requires teamwork is a great way to make new friends. My group was all crew members. I knew a few people, but I had never spoken to a majority of my group. After sailing together for a few hours we all began saying hello to each other in the hallways and hanging out together in the Crew Bar. You will likely be on this tour with people you've never met before. After working together to sail your yacht, you'll have camaraderie with them that you won't share with other guests. This bond can create friendships that may last a lifetime.

If you've been to St. Maarten before and have seen and done all that Philipsburg has to offer, consider heading out of town. St. Maarten's must see destination is commonly called Airport Beach, but is officially named Maho Beach. As its colloquial name suggests, this beach is located right next to the airport. It's actually at the end of the runway. The sand is beautiful and white and the ocean here has a sandy bottom perfect for swimming.

Check the chalkboard at Sunset Bar & Grill on the beach for the day's flight schedule. Try to stay for at least one landing and one take off. Only a narrow two-lane road separates the beach from the runway. You are so close you can feel the force of the jet engines when a plane takes off. Be prepared to get sand everywhere. And I mean everywhere. The engines turn a tranquil beach into a sandstorm. Your towel will be noticeably heavier as you leave Airport Beach because of all of the sand now lodged in it. If you have a bag with you, you will be finding sand embedded in that bag for months after your trip (What a cheap, surprise souvenir!). I also call this beach the cheapest spa you will find all cruise as each landing and departure will feel like a full body microdermabrasion. My skin has never been smoother! Make sure that your towels and other lightweight, loose items are weighted down so they won't be blown away.

Despite the precautions, Airport Beach is worth the effort. If you time it and set it up properly, you will be able to get amazing photos in this one of a kind spot. This is another unique experience that you won't find in other islands.

To get to Airport Beach, you can take a taxi (your cab driver will know it by both Airport Beach and Maho Beach. So no worries if you forget its given name.), or you could rent a car, scooter, or ATV and drive yourself there. If you have an adventurous spirit and all day, consider driving yourself. Cars are available to rent near the taxi stand at the port in Philipsburg. Consider renting a soft-top jeep so you can enjoy the sun and breeze all day. Scooters and ATVs are available for rent at various places throughout Philipsburg. I rented mine from a gentleman called Mr. Ate. He doesn't have a website, but if you exit the port area and turn right (where you would turn left to go downtown) his shop is located on the second street on the left, Grounddove Road.

> BONUS ADVICE: Renting scooters and ATVs in ports is dangerous. So dangerous your cruise line will likely discourage you from doing it. If you've never driven a scooter or an ATV, a highway in a foreign country is not a good place to start. However, if you're an experienced operator, I found that it was a great way to see the island. There is nothing separating you from your surroundings and you are free to go wherever you choose. That being said, I have seen people badly injured in accidents. Is seeing the island in this unique way worth the risk of road rash on your vacation?

When we rented jeeps or scooters and ATVs we spent the entire day cruising the island. A typical first stop was Airport Beach to watch a few planes take off and land. Along the way there are great vistas. Since we were driving ourselves, we could pull over as often as we wanted and for as long as we wanted. We always followed the beach with a visit to the French side of the island.

Lunch in Marigot is a must. Find a French café and savor your meal. After lunch you can cruise around enjoying more of the scenery or head to another beach. One of the most popular beaches on this side of the island is the clothing-optional Orient Beach.

SHOPPING

As I said, downtown Philipsburg has a plethora of shopping opportunities. In the heart of downtown, right at the end of the water taxi pier, you'll find Diamonds International and Tanzanite International. Throughout town you'll also find EFFY Jewelers, Del Sol, Cariloha, and many other options.

DINING

PHILIPSBURG

12 Metre Bar and Restaurant - Located right next to America's Cup Yacht Racing 12 Metre Challenge. I found this restaurant to be overpriced but less crowded than places further downtown. The outdoor seating and the view across Bobby's Marina and Great Bay were worth it.

Au Petit Café - Even though it's located on the Dutch side of the island, this hidden gem is a delightful French café. Walk down Front Street, the main shopping street in Philipsburg, and turn on to the side street at Colombian Emeralds International. This is Old Street and it features a restored car in the middle of the street. Au Petit Café sits a few storefronts beyond the car on the right. The crepes and omelets are fantastic. Try a can of Tropical Oasis juice. This is another European drink that I've only found this side of the Atlantic in St. Maarten. Au Petit Café was a favorite of mine for three years, but my last couple visits were not as good. There was always a delightful French chef around, but suddenly he was no longer there and the food was of a lower quality. I hope for your sake he was just on an extended vacation, because my first several meals at Au Petit Café were memorable.

The Belgian Chocolate Box by Beatrix - With a location next to the restored car on Old Street and one in the port area next to the cruise pier, you have no excuse to not try some chocolate! Beatrix offers handmade, filled chocolates, a variety of truffles, and even chocolate covered bacon. While I tried the bacon and decided it wasn't for me, I fell in love with the caramel filled waffle cookies, known as stroopwafel, dipped in chocolate. After I tried one, I couldn't go a stop in St. Maarten without picking up a package. Buy enough to snack on throughout the day, but if you want to take chocolates home, The Belgian Chocolate Box offers ship delivery so you don't need to worry about your stash melting in the Caribbean sun. Good luck not eating the whole box before the end of your cruise!

The Greenhouse - If you walk to town you'll reach The Greenhouse just after you cut through the parking lot. This restaurant has a large menu with lots of drink options and free wifi. If your ship is in late, make sure you come in for happy hour featuring 2 for 1 drinks. Cool off and try the frozen drinks.

Honky Tonk - The best beach bar in the islands! I had been coming to St. Maarten for almost a year before I discovered Honky Tonk. It's near the end of the paved beach path in the heart of Philipsburg. It's far enough that most people don't make it down there, but those who do are rewarded. Furnished with picnic tables, engulfed in loud music, and steps from the beach, you can't help but feel like you're on vacation here. Honky Tonk serves up buckets of your favorite bottles that you can take down onto the sand for a few hours of fun. Even better news: they serve Desperados!

Honky Tonk was our meeting point. If I had something to do in the morning or got off the ship alone, I knew if I made my way to Honky Tonk I would find some friends. We would eat, drink, and use the free wifi before heading down to the beach. Public restrooms are hard to find in St. Maarten so it was nice to get a pit stop with our beers too.

I tried a number of dishes at Honky Tonk and I'm the first to admit that the food is okay, but nothing spectacular. If you're looking for a good meal, go to Au Petit Café. If you're looking for some drinks, some fries, nachos, or other snacks, stop at Honky Tonk.

Pirates in Paradise - The location does not get any better than this. You'll find Pirates in Paradise located just beyond the beach and right next to the water taxi pier. It offers decent food at affordable prices.

MARIGOT

Sarafina's - Do me a favor. Head over to Google Images and type in "Sarafina's Pastry Case." Did your mouth immediately start watering? Mine did. Just thinking about all of the options and the few things I tried at Sarafina's has me ready to book a trip back to St. Maarten.

If you're headed in to Marigot this is the one place you MUST stop. Get a can of Island Oasis and a few pastries to sample. It will be one of the most memorable dining experiences of your vacation.

PERFECT DAY

On a lazy day I would walk into town for brunch at Au Petit Café. After my meal I would grab dessert at The Belgian Chocolate Box. I may walk through a few shops or out on to the beach as I head down to Honky Tonk where I would spend an afternoon enjoying the beach and refilling on snacks and Desperados as needed. I'd leave early enough to take a leisurely walk back to the ship buying my final Desperados from the man with the card table along the road.

If I was feeling adventurous, I would grab some friends and a jeep. We'd hit the road for a day of exploration, sand blasting at Airport Beach, and tasty treats on the French side.

Either way, once back on board, head up to the pool deck to watch the sail out. St. Maarten is home to beautiful sunsets!

BELOW DECK: PAYDAY

For me, everything about working on a ship was culture shock. I was in for another surprise at my first payday. I received my pay from most of my previous jobs by having the money deposited directly into my bank account or receiving a paper check. But, as you can imagine, neither of these options are very convenient if you live in the middle of the ocean. If it's deposited into your account, how do you get cash when you need it? And what good is a paper check at sea? To clear these hurdles cruise lines pay the crew in cash.

The payday process was fairly similar on every ship. We were told a time, day, and location to line up. We showed our ID in the form of a SeaPass card and were handed an envelope full of cash. We counted the cash as we moved down the line and signed a paper indicating that we had received the correct amount.

On most ships we were required to immediately pay off any charges we had incurred on our SeaPass cards since the last payday. This was colloquially known as our "Bar Bill." As you can imagine, this is an easy system in which to get into trouble. For two weeks at a time I could just swipe away throughout the ship and not have to face the financial damage until payday. The crew bar, shops, and specialty dining restaurants were all happy to accept our cards.

It takes serious self-control to be fiscally responsible while working on a cruise ship, but it is possible. I saw many crew members immediately wire home the majority of their paychecks to support their families. I managed to save enough money to travel on my vacations and eventually relocate to a new city and buy a new car when my time on ships was done. Being a crew member was one of the best financial decisions I ever made.

ST. KITTS

I've never been to the South Pacific, but this is what I imagine it looks like. St. Kitts is much more lush and green than other Caribbean islands. Take a few minutes to scan the horizon from the pier. It's a beautiful view.

When you walk through the gates at Port Zante you may be greeted by gentlemen with tiny monkeys in diapers. That probably sounds fictitious. It's not. St. Kitts is home to wild monkeys, but these are trained so tourists can pay to take a picture with one. On one of my first visits someone warned me that the monkeys have lice. I don't know if that's true or not. I never did it. I didn't want to risk it, plus it's kind of sad. I'd rather see that monkey out swinging through the jungle than wearing a diaper and sitting on my shoulder. If you decide to take a picture with one, ask the price first!

When you walk straight out from the main pier, you'll find yourself in the heart of the shopping district. This main artery bends slightly to the left where you'll go through an arched opening in the National Museum into the less touristy part of town. Walk a few blocks in to discover a large town square with a beautiful church beyond it.

I only did one tour in St. Kitts and I highly recommend it. The St. Kitts Scenic Railway allows you to experience the island in a unique way while seeing parts of the country most tourists wouldn't. We saw everything from sugar plantation ruins to black sand beaches to wild monkeys in the rainforest.

We boarded a private bus in the port area that drove us through neighboring towns and countryside to meet our train. I was expecting to be dropped off in a train station, but we ended up just waiting in a field. Soon our train was there and we took our seats on padded benches to see the island. I had been to St. Kitts several times before and it was never one of my favorite stops. This tour changed everything. St. Kitts is a beautiful island. I'm sad I only saw a small portion of it. I guess it's time to go back!

SHOPPING

All of the shopping in St. Kitts is just steps from the ship. You'll find all the classic jewelry outlets that you find in every other island. If there is a certain piece you are looking for, stop in and check out the selection.

DINING

Domino's Pizza - It is located just beyond the port area near the large park with a church on the edge. It is further than most guests venture and it offers what you would expect. Same chain, and food, as in the United States.

Rituals Coffee House - Rituals appeared in the middle of my visits to St. Kitts. It was brand new and undiscovered by the rest of the crew so I loved the relaxed and uncrowded atmosphere. Located across the street from Domino's, I recommend this spot if you're looking for a place with wifi, pastries, and a large variety of drinks. They serve up everything from coffee shop style beverages to milkshakes.

Scoops - This ice cream shop is located right in the main port area on one of the side streets to the left of the main artery. The ice cream is pricey, but delicious!

Sweet Lime - The first place you see when you get off the ship. Sweet Lime is upstairs in MaPau Casino. Enjoy your food while lounging on couches, looking over the harbor, and surfing the free wifi.

PERFECT DAY

I would hop off early and head to Rituals for a pastry and morning coffee. Then I'd take a walk around the park before heading back to the pier to meet my tour group. The afternoon would be spent on the St. Kitts Scenic Railway circumnavigating the island. I'd return to Port Zante in time for a bit of shopping and maybe a pre-dinner snack at Scoops.

BELOW DECK: PARTY TIME

Guests on a cruise experience different theme parties nearly every night. About once a month the crew gets to have a theme party. Toga, Superheroes, Back to School, Pirates, and Safety* were just a few of the themes we had.

The different divisions on the ship (Entertainment, Food and Beverage, Spa, etc.) take turns hosting the parties. The division in charge for the month comes up with the theme, location, and decorations. Most parties take place in the crew bar, but every few months a guest area was closed for a few hours late one night to allow the crew to use the space. We sometimes got to use the nightclub or even one of the upper, outer decks. On one ship they closed down the kid's pool area and the crew got to use the waterslide.

Some of the crew came in costume, but everyone was welcome. Even better than the costumes were the free drinks. There were usually a few different beers, sodas, and maybe some wine. I was also on a ship that got really into Jell-O shots so we had a few parties in a row with those.

The crew party nights were the most social. Everyone had a reason to be out. The party was for all of us so we all got together to celebrate our ship and our hard work. And the free booze.

*A Safety Party usually involved lifejackets, fluorescent vests, and a variety of personal protective equipment including gloves and goggles.

ANTIGUA

The pier will once again deliver you into the heart of downtown shopping. As you reach the end of the pier, take the boardwalk to your right for a quieter stroll along the water. This route will eventually weave its way back into town as well. All roads lead to shopping!

If you decide to stick around town and do some shopping, leave time to explore and be sure to visit St. John's Cathedral also known as St. John the Divine. This cathedral is located just a few blocks back from the main shopping district. You can see the facade of St. John's Cathedral looming over the city as your ship pulls into port. The over 150-year-old church was under repair during my visit, but it was still well worth the trip.

Antigua has beautiful beaches. I only visited the nearby Runaway and Dickenson Bays, but after you visit you'll see why I didn't need to go anywhere else. The white sand beaches meet the clear turquoise waters, convincing me this must be heaven on earth.

There is a Sandals Resort located in Dickenson Bay. We walked through their beach area, but were asked to leave if we tried to settle there since we were not resort guests. Don't worry, there's plenty of room to either side on this beach and it's all gorgeous. As in other islands, you may need to pay to use a chair or umbrella.

> BONUS ADVICE: If someone offers to help you with your chair or umbrella, you will be expected to tip them. Early on in my career I naively thought they were just being friendly. In some spots I wasn't even allowed to rearrange the chairs on my own. If I started moving a chair, someone immediately showed up to "help" me.

If the beach is too relaxing and you need some adrenaline, check out the Antigua Rainforest Zipline Tours. At the time of the tour I was afraid of heights and had a recent bad experience at a ropes course, but I'm so glad I didn't let my fear stop me!

The day started with a safety briefing in the offices of Antigua

Rainforest Zipline Tours. Then everyone got outfitted with the gear we needed: helmets, gloves, trolleys, and lanyards. We crossed a short swinging bridge and we were ready for our first zip.

Each zipline is made of two cables as a backup precaution. There was a guide at each station to hook me onto the line. The guides showed me how to "hand brake" as well. One hand loosely glides along the cable behind the trolley and squeezes when it's time to stop (hence the gloves). I could see everything that was happening and knew I was safe. The hardest part was taking the first step off the first platform. After that everything was just a blurry blast!

The ziplines crisscrossed their way through the canopy of the rainforest. After several zips of varying lengths, it was time for the Challenge Course. This was a low ropes course with elements of balance, strength, and in my case, courage. I conquered every element and had a great experience.

The Antigua Rainforest Zipline Tour was a great way to get out in nature, explore in a different ecosystem, and have some fun. It ended with a visit to the gift shop. They took some photos of us zipping along and those were available for purchase. Every participant was awarded a Certificate of Bravery. I know it's a carbon copy award they give everyone, but as someone who had to face her fears and step out of her comfort zone, I displayed it proudly in my cabin for weeks to come.

On another trip I somehow convinced my friend Brian to go on an island tour with me. This isn't something crew members do. A vast majority of us wanted good food and fast internet. Once those needs were satisfied it was time to find a beach. But, for some reason we decided to hire a taxi for the day and our driver told us about Antigua as he drove us across the island. He showed us the historic area of Nelson's Dockyard and the panoramic view from Shirely Heights. Neither is to be missed, but the view from Shirely Heights is especially memorable.

I don't know how I heard about it, but I wanted to visit Devil's Bridge. Our driver told us that lots of slaves came to this spot because there was nothing between here and West Africa. They would sit and talk to their families back home or if things got really bad they committed suicide by throwing themselves into the water. The shape, depth, and rough waters of this cove made it so anyone who went in could not make it back out alive. For that reason it is not recommended that anyone attempt to cross the bridge. If you make it part way across and a wave knocks you into the water, it's all over. But we'd come all this way and we were young and stupid. Yep, we both crossed it! And posed for pictures in the middle. Possibly not the smartest move either of us has ever made, but we both knew it would be a great story.

In the area of Devil's Bridge we caught a rare glimpse of a mongoose. In over three years in the Caribbean, I only saw another one in Jamaica. Both were fleeting looks.

SHOPPING

The main shopping district is, again, at the end of the pier. You'll find all the standard jewelry chains you will begin to recognize from other islands.

For a change of pace, check out The Best of Books Bookstore located just a few blocks back on St. Mary's Street. It's a crowded store with seemingly endless nooks stuffed full of books. I consider this another "slice of life" location. It's less of a tourist spot and more for the locals.

My favorite Antiguan purchase is Ting. This grapefruit flavored soda is manufactured in Jamaica and only found on a few islands. It was a common beverage in Antigua so I would use the abundance as an opportunity to stock up. I'd buy at least three extra bottles to take back on board.

DINING

There are a number of restaurants straight off the ship in the main shopping district of town. Several of these places have televisions and a sports bar feel. I was on a ship that called here on Sundays and these places would be packed with guests trying to watch their favorite American football teams.

BONUS ADVICE: Go on a cruise to relax and spend time with those you love, not to watch sports. There is a decent chance that whatever team or sporting event you feel you must watch won't be shown on your ship. On the ships I was on we showed three NFL games on Sundays and the NFL chose which games we received. We couldn't get coverage of the Olympics, I never saw a hockey game, only select college games were shown, and Premier League soccer was blacked out. Literally. The channel would be playing as normal, it would say the game was about to start, and then the screen would go blank until the game ended. Sports leagues request enormous licensing fees for their games and some ships may not have the game you want. I once received a post cruise comment along the lines of, "I never would have come on this cruise if I had known you wouldn't be showing the _____ game." If it's a game you absolutely must see, book your vacation in the off-season.

Big Banana: #1 Pizza in the Caribbean! This is my favorite lunch spot in all of the islands. It beats out Shipwreck in St. Thomas, Honky Tonk in St. Maarten, and Pizza e Birra in San Juan. If you only get off the ship for one meal your entire cruise, get off in Antigua and head to Big Banana. Follow the boardwalk to the right at the end of the pier then follow the path back towards town. I always ordered a pepperoni and bacon pizza with a Ting to drink. I was never disappointed.

Well, that's not true. I was actually repeatedly disappointed when I realized my ship was in Antigua on Sundays and Big Banana is closed on Sundays. It was heartbreaking. I didn't want to eat anywhere else; I knew it wouldn't compare. In fact I was so fixated on Big Banana one weekend that my boyfriend actually took me to the one in the airport on the other side of the island. We both agreed, it was worth the drive!

Australian Homemade: What better to wash down your pizza with than waffles and ice cream? Located just around the corner from Big Banana, these freshly made Belgian waffles topped with rapidly melting ice cream make an unforgettable end to your meal.

Hemingways Caribbean Cafe: I ate here on one of my very first trips. I waited an hour for a sandwich and never returned. I don't recall anything about the food, just the wait.

PERFECT DAY

Big Banana opens at 11:00 am and I would be there right as it opened. After enjoying my pizza and Ting, it would be time to hop in a cab and head to the beach. I'd spend the rest of the afternoon relaxing in the sun and playing in clear waters. After heading back to the port I'd stop at Australian Homemade for a waffle and ice cream. I'd make one last stop for a few bottles of Ting to last me until I was here again.

BELOW DECK: SECURITY

My new office recently instituted a policy where all employees need to scan their ID badge before the elevator will work. This is seen as an inconvenience to many of my colleagues, but it seems so laughably trivial to me. When I was working on the ship I had to scan my ID, remove my shoes, have all of my items scanned, and sometimes present my passport before I was allowed to go ashore. When it was time to come back I had to show my ID at the gate on the pier to get in line for my ship. Once I crossed the gangway I had to scan my ID, remove my shoes, and have all of my items scanned. I had to walk through a metal detector and in some ports all of the crew were given full body pat downs. Once on board I had another card to scan to get access to my office.

You, as a guest, won't encounter a process quite so rigorous, but remember the ship's security team has a large job to tackle and they're there to keep you safe. Patience and smile goes a long way with them.

DOMINICA

Not to be confused with the Dominican Republic, Dominica is a beautiful island all on its own. Ships dock in the town of Roseau and this is the perfect day to take a tour. There are a few shops, a local craft market, a farmers market, and a couple of restaurants in town. But not enough to keep guests occupied for an entire day. The countryside surrounding Roseau is worth the trip out of town.

I took a couple river tubing trips in Dominica. The island is known as the "Land of 365 Rivers," so it was great to take time to see a few. I met my guide and my group on the pier where we were escorted to a van and driven to our launch site. There we received some instructions, a life vest, a tube, a paddle, and a helmet. We left our bags in the van with everything that couldn't get wet (towel, clothes, wallets, etc.), so plan ahead. I never had any trouble, but I certainly wouldn't want to leave many valuables in the van all day.

Once on the Layou River, we simply floated downstream. We used our paddles to push ourselves off rocks or get us through slow sections. They also came in handy when my group of friends was trying to link up to go downstream together. We'd extend the paddle towards the adrift friend. They'd grab on, we'd pull them in and hang on to each other's tubes as we went along.

There were a few guides with us to make sure the group stayed together and no one got left behind. If we were approaching dangerous rapids or a shallow part of the river, the guides would stand by the area where we shouldn't go and push us away from the trouble spots.

We spent well over an hour on the river floating past the local flora and fauna. Some parts of the river were gentle and relaxing while other portions had rapids that spun and splashed us. In the end we were rewarded with rum punch.

This is one of my favorite tours in the Caribbean, but remember that it is an adventure sport and there are dangers. On one of my trips a guest ran into a rock and his elbow was badly cut and bloodied. I recommend this tour for people in good physical shape who are used to and enjoy being out in nature.

Dominica is known for beautiful dive sites, but I wasn't yet a certified diver during my calls there. However, I had a great snorkel trip to Champagne Reef. The reef gets its name from the sensation of swimming through a glass of champagne that you feel when you're over the reef. Gasses continuously bubble and rise from vents in the ocean floor making this a truly unique site. Aside from the fun of the bubbles there is also lots of sea life to discover. The most memorable find on my trip was a pufferfish.

Champagne Reef is only a ten-minute drive from Roseau. If your ship does not offer tours there, check out Champagne Reef Dive and Snorkel. You can book a snorkel package with round trip transportation from your ship for around $40.

If both the river rafting and the Champagne Reef snorkel trip sound too adventurous for you, consider doing an island tour. Your ship will offer a variety. Look for one that will take you to Emerald Pool, Sulfur Springs, and Trafalgar Falls for beautiful scenery. The tours I was on required a bit of hiking after a van ride to each destination. Most of these sights are not visible from the road. Check with your ship or tour company with accessibility questions.

If you end up getting off the ship late or spending a majority of your day in Roseau, but would still like to see some nature, take a short walk to the Botanical Gardens. The gardens are not as impressive as the sites outside of town, but it is better than nothing if you are short on time.

SHOPPING

As I said, your options are limited here. I would save the shopping for St. Thomas or St. Maarten and book an excursion in Dominica. Diamonds are nice, but the real treasure here is the beauty of the island.

DINING

I tried a few different places around Roseau, but there were no stand out winners. There is a Kentucky Fried Chicken (popular in the Caribbean) over by the Roseau River. It's located near the local market where you can pick up fresh fruits and vegetables.

PERFECT DAY

All of the tours that I mentioned are great and memorable. If I find myself back in Dominica I would probably head back to Champagne Reef for a unique experience I've never found anywhere else. If I were feeling ambitious, I would see the reef in the morning then spend the afternoon on the river. But I could just as easily spend all day on an island tour soaking in the beauty of Dominica. The key is to get out of Roseau. There's a lot more to the island than what you see when you walk off the ship. Book a tour and go explore!

BELOW DECK: SAFETY DUTIES

Crew members are not just on board to fulfill the duties in their job descriptions. It is their job to pay attention and put safety first so the guests can relax and have a great time. The emphasis on safety begins the first day crew members join a ship as they all must attend Pre-Departure Safety Training before the ship sails. This training lasts a couple hours and goes over the types and operation of fire extinguishers, what to do in emergency situations, how to operate fire doors and watertight doors, how to launch a life raft, and a review of the ship's emergency code words. New hires, or crew members beginning their first contract, are put through a much more rigorous training process that lasts for weeks. As a new hire I used a fire hose for the first (and only) time and was taught how to flip over a life raft if an unmanned one was floating upside down. Every five years crew members are recertified in Crowd Management. On a ship with thousands of guests, this is a crucial skill. It's all about clear communication and staying calm. The ship's officers and crew take safety very seriously. We know that everyone on board is counting on us to keep them safe and we will do everything we can to ensure that we do.

In addition to the trainings there is a weekly safety drill. Each crew member is given an Emergency Number and each number has certain duties assigned to it. Over the years I was a life raft launcher, a lifeboat loading assistant, an assistant lifeboat captain, and a Communications Officer. We train for these responsibilities and practice them often.

On some ships I also had to report Safety Observations, which made me look critically at everything and see how I could make it safer. I reported doors that slammed, items in hallways that could impede traffic flow in an emergency, and rugs that were trip hazards.

The skills I learned are something I carry with me everyday. I constantly notice unsafe situations and try to make them better. Last year I was at an event in a large auditorium when one of the guests had a medical emergency. I immediately went into response mode as other patrons looked around wondering what to do. Ship's staff are highly trained. We are leaders who take action when necessary. Our top priority is your safety so your top priority can be a great vacation.

ST. LUCIA

Most ships dock in Castries, St Lucia. I've been here a handful of times and found the town of Castries lackluster. This is another great island to book a tour.

One of the main attractions in St. Lucia is The Pitons. For my first viewing of The Pitons, my boyfriend and a friend of ours found a local tour operator selling tours on his boat to guests from our ship. When he had enough people, we set off around the island. The sail was relaxing and the guide, knowledgeable.

We had a great view of The Pitons from the water, but we also had a land portion to our tour. Our captain double-parked in Soufriere and we climbed out of our boat, across the deck of another boat, and onto the pier. I wonder how the other boat's captain felt about this arrangement?

Once on land, we traveled by van to St. Lucia's Drive-in Volcano. I was pumped to see a volcano! I had been picturing red-hot lava spewing wildly into the air or flowing down a mountain and across the road. In reality it looked like a large crater with steam rising from it. It was cool, but not full of the epic excitement I had dreamed.

Back on the boat, we sailed into Marigot Bay and our guide informed us that this was used as a filming location for the original "Doctor Dolittle" film. We docked here and were told to go try the local restaurants before returning to the boat at a certain time. We looked around and quickly decided on Dolittle's Restaurant and Bar in the Marigot Beach Club and Dive Resort. We enjoyed our meal and as we were paying our bill, we looked up to see our tour boat sailing away. My friends started yelling and waving, but the boat didn't turn around or even stop. In a panic, we ran back to the pier where our boat had been. We didn't really know where we were on the island or how long a cab would take for us to get back. What if we missed the ship?

When we got to the Marigot Bay dock there was, thankfully, another boat headed back to our ship so we hopped on with them. We caught up to our original boat and they made us jump from one to the other while in the middle of the water! In the end, we made it back before the All On Board time and avoided a disaster (Well, nearly avoided a disaster. My friends were both late to work and got written warnings in their personnel files. If we had missed the ship however, we would have likely all been fired.). It may sound like "All's well that ends well," but in reality the unnecessary stress has really clouded the happy memories of that day. I wish we had just paid more and gone on a tour through the ship.

> BONUS ADVICE: This is a perfect example of why to take a tour your ship offers instead of booking it on your own. If we had been on the ship's tour they would have counted the guests before leaving Marigot Bay and re-alized they were missing us. Sometimes your peace of mind is worth the extra dollars you will spend on a tour.

On a later visit to St. Lucia I did a ship sponsored Sail and Snor-kel tour. This tour included a sail on a spacious catamaran, sights of The Pitons, and a beach break to snorkel, swim, and do jumps and flips off the boat into the water. It was much more relaxing knowing that my group wouldn't leave me behind this time.

SHOPPING

Your options are extremely limited here. While the immediate port area has some shops, I recommend shopping in other ports and booking a tour in St. Lucia.

DINING

CASTRIES

Auberge Seraphine - If you do stick around the port area, schedule a lunch stop here. I'm sure any cab driver can easily take you here from the port or you can walk there along the road. I received direc-tions from some friends that involved the following: "Find the dirt path on the other side of the port. Climb through the hole in the fence and keep following the path down the hill. Then follow the road along the water and you can't miss it. It's a big white building with a pond out front. No, I don't know the name of it." It's a miracle I ever found the place. Climbing through the hole in the fence definitely sounded like a trap. I thought I would never be seen or heard from again once I attempted this journey. But it all worked out. You should probably take a cab.

I typically ordered the turkey club sandwich and was never disappointed. The Auberge Seraphine is a restaurant and hotel so there is free wifi. After lunch we always used the pool upstairs. I don't know if we were allowed to as the general public, as restaurant customers, or because we were crew members. Regardless, give it a try. The rooftop pool is small, but quiet and relaxing with great views of the port.

MARIGOT BAY

Dolittle's Restaurant and Bar - Despite the stressful events that happened after my meal here, I really liked the atmosphere. The service was slow (so slow I missed my boat), so plan ahead.

PERFECT DAY

You really can't go all the way to St. Lucia and not see The Pitons. Have a look at the ship's tours and find the one that sounds right for you. There will be Land and Sea tours as well as Sail and Snorkel tours. You'll have lots of options. Have a great time and a stress-free day knowing the ship knows where you are and you won't get left behind.

BELOW DECK: RELIEF WORK

Most of us think of cruise ships as floating cities of fun. I had never considered the help they could provide to areas local to the ports. The largest example of this came after the 2010 earthquake in Haiti.

At the time I had only been at sea for a couple months so I was a very new crew member. The ship I was on frequently called on Royal Caribbean's Private Destination of Labadee in Haiti. There was much discussion over whether or not ships should be visiting Labadee when towns and lives were in chaos just a few miles away. In the end it was decided we would go. Haiti needed our business now more than ever and we could bring supplies.

Every available free space on the ship became a cargo area. My ship alone delivered several pallets of crutches and walkers. We donated mattresses. We held clothing and food drives as well as fundraisers. In one cruise alone we delivered 29,000 servings of food. On that same cruise we delivered the only medical oxygen generator in the country. Prior to its arrival, patients needed to be bagged during surgery. This sometimes led to complications and also required another medical professional to be in the room who otherwise could be off helping someone else.

Royal Caribbean's decision to return to Haiti so quickly was a controversial one and I understand the concerns. But I for one, as a person who was there, am grateful for the commitment they showed to a country in need and for the way our guests and crew were willing to help out in any way we could.

BARBADOS

Barbados is the perfect beach day and one of my favorite stops. This former United Kingdom colony also has beautiful sights and a large downtown to explore.

Ships dock at the Bridgetown cruise port. Some of the slips are a long way from the terminal. On days when many ships call on Barbados, a shuttle bus service runs back and forth to the far slips all day. While convenient, it slows the process down. Hopefully you'll be docked close!

The taxi stand is on the far side of the terminal. Many taxis are larger vans and passengers may have to wait until the vehicle fills up before the driver will want to leave.

If you would rather walk into town, head past the taxi stand, out the gate, and onto a paved path along the water to the right. Follow this beautiful path through a park and over a cement bridge. Look down as you cross the bridge and you're likely to see crabs scurrying about. The walk after the park always felt a bit sketchy for a few blocks, but I never had any problems. After you pass the bus terminal, you will see the water on your right again. Cut through the parking lot and up onto the boardwalk. Here you'll find benches to relax on and views of Constitution River. Take some time to look into the river - you might spot a turtle swimming along.

When it comes to having a good day in Barbados, look no further than The Boatyard. The Boatyard is my #1 favorite beach in the entire Caribbean. There is an entrance fee, but it includes beach chairs, umbrellas, sunbeds, rope swing into the ocean, ocean trampoline, a drink, and even transportation back to the ship. Spend your day sunning, swimming, eating, and drinking. When you work up your courage, jump off the pier or fly off the rope swing. I have great memories of this place!

When you're on the beach at The Boatyard, if you walk away from town (left, when facing the ocean) you'll see a large double-decker boat come and go from the shore. Beyond the boat is a buoy line. If you wait in this area you'll see dive boats arrive about 100-200 yards from the shore. A bunch of people will jump in the water with masks and snorkels. This area has a couple of awesome shipwrecks and the guides on the boats feed the sea turtles to bring them closer to the tourists.

The large groups of people will point you in the right direction, but it can get very crowded and chaotic with everyone in the water at once. The good thing about not being on the tour is you don't have to leave when everyone else does. Be patient and hang back a bit. The shipwreck will still be there when the group is done, but stay close when it's time to see the turtles as they'll begin to disperse after the feeding stops.

A friend of mine found this spot when he saw this happening. He took me there and we swam out. It's a significant swim. Don't try this if you're not a strong swimmer in good physical shape. The water is deep and you'll be floating and swimming for a while. The effort is worth it though. The sunken ship is larger than most wrecks I've seen. In addition, there were lots of fish to observe. The tourists' boats move closer to the shore for turtle time. You'll be spent after this swim, but it's a Caribbean highlight for me. Of course, you can always book the tour for a guide and a less physically demanding experience. Also, book the tour if you don't have your own snorkel gear.

On some of my first trips, my ship visited Barbados on Sunday. One week I decided to go to church. I walked a slightly scary route to Berean Bible Church. Everyone was so friendly. Before the service they all welcomed me, greeted me, showed me to a Sunday School class, and had lots of questions for me. I was settling in nicely and was enjoying observing all that was happening around me when suddenly, in the middle of service, they announced that they had a visitor. They asked me to stand and the entire congregation sang me a welcome song. I've visited a lot of churches in my life, and this is the only one that sang to me. It was crazy, uncomfortable, but memorable. After the service a couple of expat Brits gave me a ride back to the ship. I always talk about trying to see an authentic side to the islands and this was the most authentic experience I had.

BONUS ADVICE: Don't tell your mom you got into a car with two strangers.

I was so in love with The Boatyard I never felt the need to go anywhere else. However, three of my friends rented a car one time to go check out the rest of the island. I'm not sure where they rented the car from, but they ended up getting in an accident. The car wasn't drivable so they couldn't return it. They eventually flagged down a cab to bring them back to the ship, but it was too late. We had already left. The port agent loaded them onto the pilot boat that was coming to meet the ship and the guys had to climb up a ladder hung on the side of the ship and in through the open shell gate doors. I was there when they got on board and it was terrifying. They were relieved to have made it back, but were still in danger of losing their jobs. In the end they all kept their jobs, were given warnings, and we all got a strong reminder about leaving extra time to make it back to the ship. As a guest, you won't have the option of bringing another boat to the ship. The port agent will meet you and help you make arrangements to meet the ship at an upcoming port of call. You will be responsible for all associated costs.

SHOPPING

The cruise terminal has many shopping options. As does downtown Bridgetown. You'll find many of the stores you've grown accustomed to seeing in the Caribbean plus a few more. There's also a mall downtown with additional shopping opportunities.

DINING

Cruise Terminal - The terminal has a great bar and smoothie location to the right of where you enter to get back to the ship. There's also a little place that serves food with picnic tables outside. My friends love the macaroni and cheese here and it is a very convenient spot to stop for a quick bite when getting on or off the ship.

The Boatyard - Have I mentioned how great The Boatyard is? It's great. Trust me. Actually, no. Don't trust me. Go try it for yourself. The yellow hot sauce served here is amazing on french fries. And the orange juice is the best I've ever tasted. The Boatyard has tons of drink options. Just squeeze your way up to the bar and shout out your order.

PERFECT DAY

Do I even need to say it? I'd go to The Boatyard! I'd likely get off the ship early and walk through town, looking for turtles in the river. I'd get an orange juice upon entering The Boatyard and spend the day laying in the sun, swimming, jumping off the pier, and hopefully trying out the rope swing. After a hot sauce covered lunch, I'd walk along the shore then swim out to find the shipwrecks and the turtles. I'd take the free transport back to the ship and pause on the pier to listen to a local band that is typically stationed there.

BELOW DECK: VACATION MODE

We all do it. We get into relaxation mode and switch our brains off. On the ship we called it "checking your brain at the gangway" and most guests were guilty of it.

The best example I ever saw of this happened on my first Christmas Eve at sea. I was on the Royal Promenade (the "Main Street" of the ship) and had just finished filming our entertainment staff and guests singing Christmas carols. A guest approached me and asked, "What time is the midnight mass?" I paused and looked at him trying to think of an answer that wouldn't make him feel dumb. Eventually I said, "I believe it's at twelve o'clock."

Kick back, relax, enjoy your trip, but try to maintain your common sense.

CURAÇAO

One of my favorite parts about the ABC islands (Aruba, Bonaire, and Curaçao) is their European influence. It's noticeable everywhere you look. Nowhere is it more obvious than in the colorful skyline of Willemstad. At first glance you will think you're in the Netherlands.

The port area has some great shopping and even a casino steps from your ship. If you didn't donate enough onboard, the good people of Curaçao will take some more. A few steps further is Rif Fort. Take a stroll through this historic fort now populated with places to shop, eat, and drink. Much of the port area was under construction while I was visiting with new stores opening weekly. It was really shaping up and I'm certain it is now a destination all on its own.

No matter how great you find the port area, don't let convenience stop you from heading downtown. In fact the highlight of your trip might be getting there. Take a walk across the floating bridge! Not only can you marvel at the European inspired skyline from the bridge, but the bridge itself is a bit of a marvel. Ships frequently have to navigate this channel in order to get into Willemstad Harbor so this bridge detaches and swings open as the traffic passes. It's a fun experience to be on the bridge as this happens, or even just to see it happen. It is, however, less fun when you're trying to get from one side to the other quickly and the bridge is not passable. A ferry service replaces the bridge when it is impassable. The ferries sail from near the entrances to the bridge. They are smaller, crowded, and more time consuming. As always, make sure you leave extra time to get back to the ship.

When you reach downtown, take some time to explore the floating market. It is essentially a farmers market, but all of the stalls are boats docked along the riverbank on the edge of town. It's a unique and enjoyable experience.

I went diving with CURious2Dive on my last visit to Curaçao. The dive and the guide, Hans, were fantastic. I especially enjoyed the end of the dive when we got to explore a sunken tugboat. Standing on the deck of a sunken ship was a strange feeling. The dive package was meant to include a download link to pictures taken during the dive, but I never received that link. Overall, it was still a great experience.

SHOPPING

More of the same here again. There are shops in the little port area just off the ship and many more when you head downtown. Though definitely not as glamorous, save some time to check out the floating market.

DINING

Denny's - If you feel like heading away from the tourist side of town, head to Denny's. Home of the same comfort food the chain is popular for in the United States, Denny's is the opposite direction of all of the shopping. The walk is along a sidewalk next to a marsh and is another "slice of life" moment. You're in the real Curaçao when you're over there.

Sopranos - This little piano/sports bar is located in Rif Fort in the section of town between your ship and the floating bridge. The food and the atmosphere were good. They had some of the fastest internet in the Caribbean.

European Food - You will find European influence throughout Willemstad. French, Italian, and German cuisine abound. Many places have outdoor seating. Find a spot with a view and try something new!

PERFECT DAY

I only got to go diving in Curaçao once, so I would like to do that again when I go back. The visibility was great and there was a lot to see. Curaçao is a beautiful island and it just gets better under the surface.

BELOW DECK: BEHIND THE FORBIDDEN DOOR

If you've been on a cruise you've likely seen crew members disappear through nondescript doors marked "Crew Only." Behind these doors lies a magical maze of a world simply called the "Crew Area." I would love to tell you that all of the glitz, glamor, and excess that the guests see and experience everyday carries over to the crew areas, but it doesn't. The best word to describe these spaces is "industrial." As a rule of thumb, if you enter a hallway or stairway that is not carpeted, you're likely in a crew area. Everything is metal. Metal doors, metal steps, metal handrails, metal walls. Metal. Everywhere.

What the crew areas lack in aesthetics they make up for in convenience. In these areas we didn't need to wear nametags or be in uniform. The crew areas were essentially our neighborhood, our homes, while the rest of the ship was our office. Everything we needed was in these hallways from our cabins to our dining room, called the "mess." We even had a crew gym and a store for supplies and snacks called the "Slop Chest."

By far the most popular spot in the crew areas was the crew bar known as "Back Deck." On many ships this was an open air space at the back of the ship, but on some ships it is an indoor room and on others it is at the front of the ship. Regardless of the location, "Back Deck" is a term that stuck. The bars in the guest areas may have a better atmosphere, but the drinks at the crew bar were about three times cheaper. Beer was cheaper than water as a Corona cost $0.97 and a bottle of water cost $1.50. Most cocktails were around $3.00 and shots were a dollar or two. A few nights ago I had a shot with my friends at a restaurant near my apartment that cost me as much as an entire night at the crew bar.

It's a different world in the crew areas. Many cruise lines now offer behind the scenes tours that will show you these spaces. Don't try to sneak in and explore them. As crew, we know our own. If you don't belong, someone will immediately recognize it and ask you to leave.

ARUBA

Part of the ABC islands (Aruba, Bonaire, and Curaçao), Aruba is the Deep South of the Caribbean. In fact, it's so far south it's practically in South America. Lather on your sunscreen, you're going to need it here!

I've been to Aruba a handful of times and one of my favorite activities was a simple walk through town. After getting off the ship you only need to endure a few city blocks before you're out next to the water again. The sidewalk soon gives way to a boardwalk. After the marina, you can turn into a little shopping area where you'll pass a casino before reaching a bench lined path along the water's edge. I spent many hours here relaxing, reading, and watching various exotic wildlife such as lizards and iguanas. This path follows the water and leads to other parks. I always enjoyed the tiny little park between the marina and the ocean.

The only tour I ever took in Aruba was to De Palm Island, a private, all-inclusive waterpark destination. I loved De Palm so much I came back months later on a different ship. A visit here is expensive, but food and drinks are included and there are a variety of activities to try. If you have a full day the price really isn't that bad.

De Palm Island is a few miles outside of town. If you haven't arranged a trip there through your ship you will need to take a cab or you can book transportation with the resort. Check in at the ticket booth in the parking lot then board a ferry to the island. When it's time to go back to the ship, make sure you leave extra time for any ferry or transport delays.

Don't get too excited about the waterpark portion of De Palm Island. It's small. It is awesome for kids, and still fun for us "big kids." If the waterpark isn't exciting enough, you can go for a ride on a banana boat behind a jet ski. Or play basketball. Or volleyball. Or take a dance lesson. Or visit the buffet. Or the snack bar. Or the bar. Or lay on the beach. There's so much to do on this tiny island!

Make sure you leave time to snorkel. The crew at De Palm outfitted me with mask, snorkel, fins, and life vest. I've snorkeled in many islands, but this was some of the best. So many fish and lots of different habitats to explore. The parrotfish is a must see. And you will see them. You will probably see many of them. These multicolored fish reminded me of Donkey from the *Shrek* films. You have to see one to know why. The water here was a bit rougher than in other, more protected, places I've snorkeled so I was grateful for the vest.

SHOPPING

Aruba has all of the standard Caribbean jewelry stores. It is home to many tax and duty free shops. There are also several open air malls featuring familiar brands.

DINING

Dunkin' Donuts - If you're from the Northeast US and are really missing your coffee, you are in luck in Aruba. As an added bonus, one of the shops has an in house Baskin-Robbins. Just in case you weren't getting enough calories from those buffets....

Iguana Joes - I can't recall what I ordered here, but I remember the fun, bright atmosphere. The restaurant is on the second story and the open air seating offers great opportunities for people watching.

Starbucks - Time for another caffeine fix? Aruba can help you with that. There is a Starbucks in the Renaissance hotel as well as one across the street next to the marina.

PERFECT DAY

My favorite days were spent at De Palm Island. I would love to get a big group of my friends together again and go spend the day there. There's something for everyone and it's impossible to be bored.

BELOW DECK: A NIGHT TO REMEMBER

The best place to be on the ship after dark is the bow. On most ships this is the helipad. The bridge looks over the helipad so at night it is completely dark as to not impair the bridge officers' vision. That makes this the perfect place for stargazing. On some ships this is a crew only area and on others there is a crew only area just behind it.

I spent the majority of one contract in Europe with a home port of Barcelona. My friends and I started buying bottles of cava in port for a few Euros apiece and bringing them back on board. If you're sailing as a guest, that's not possible. Any alcohol you buy in port is stored for you until you're ready to depart the ship. But at the time, crew could buy bottles in port and bring it back to our cabins. When it came to the cava in Barcelona, we bought as much as we could carry.

Late in my contract there was a meteor shower forecasted and my friends and I gathered all the cava we had left and headed out to the crew area behind the helipad. We spent hours staring at the stars while drinking cava in our deck chairs. Friends from the United States, United Kingdom, Hungary, Columbia, Brazil, and other places from around the globe surrounded me. I was content and knew this would be one of the most special moments of my life. I was humbled then, and still am now, to realize what a crazy, beautiful life I was living.

PRIVATE DESTINATIONS

Most of today's major cruise lines sail to Private Destinations. Private Destinations are ports were only your ship or ships from your cruise line's brand will dock. You won't find Carnival alongside Norwegian or Princess alongside MSC. Instead, this port is essentially an extension of your ship. You'll find the same staff that has been serving you onboard now out here. All drinks, tours, and spa treatments will be available for purchase with your SeaPass card. Even better, things like food and beach chairs are included. Childcare is available on the property as an extension of the service offered onboard.

I have experience with Royal Caribbean so I will only speak directly to those ports. Check with your cruise line for more information.

LABADEE

Located on the northern coast of Haiti, Labadee offers an adventure-filled day in the sun. Once a tendering port, a nice, new pier is now in place. This allows multiple ships to call on Labadee at once and for guests to walk straight off the ship and get to the beach without the hassle of taking another boat to shore.

Labadee is most known for its adrenaline rush inducing zipline; billed the "Longest Zipline Over Water." The views from the top are so magnificent you have to try it at least once. The harnesses are well designed and it actually feels like you are simply just sitting down as opposed to hanging by a cable. I was afraid of heights at the time, but decided to just give it a try and I discovered how safe it really was.

We started our day with a safety briefing and instructions for putting on our harnesses. After we were all suited up we headed to a much smaller zipline inland to tryout what we learned. For example, to go slower we needed to "starfish" or spread our arms and legs wide. After we conquered the little run, we were bussed up to the top of the main zipline. The staff is well-trained and very helpful. I was always tied off and never had any fear of falling. They hooked me on to the line and sent me on my way.

Prepare yourself for the ending. Depending on how fast you are going, you may have a very aggressive stop. I've seen people hit the end so hard that their feet flew up over their head and above the cable. True confession: watching people stop is so entertaining I used to eat lunch at a picnic table overlooking the end of the zipline. Lunch and a show. Even funnier, there are photographers from the ship positioned at the end of the run. I'm sure they've captured some gems over the years! Fortunately, my stopping experience was nothing crazy, but it was a bit sad. I had held my camera the entire journey and was recording video. The abrupt stop at the end caused me to nearly drop my camera and when I caught it I accidentally shut it off and lost the whole movie I had just shot. Sad. Despite the sad ending, the view and the feeling of flying were worth it.

A couple of Labadee's newest features are the roller coaster and the waterslide. I was among the first group of people to ever ride the rollercoaster, perhaps even before it was open to the public. It's unlike anything I had ever experienced in amusement parks. The cars look similar to go-carts, hold up to two passengers, and include hand-brakes to slow down as necessary. The more weight in the car, the faster it goes. In fact, I remember being in a car with my friend Vince and he held my hands down so I couldn't pull the brake. The ride itself is great fun and you can go at your own pace so it is a great activity for a parent and child. As an added bonus, there are amazing views from several places on the track.

The waterslide is located on the other side of the peninsula. Hopefully they've made some modifications to this because I was unimpressed with my trip down the slide. There was very little water running down it and I had to push myself along to avoid getting stuck. There were always lots of kids around and they seemed to love it.

The Snorkel Safari tour is the only trip I took off the mainland. I was surprised by how much there was to see around Labadee. Most of the beaches are sandy, but after I took a boat several hundred yards offshore, the sea floor was covered in life. The tour includes mask, snorkel, inflatable snorkel vest, instruction, and an in-water guide to point out and identify sea life.

If you're looking to snorkel from shore, stick to the side of the island with the water slide and aqua park. This area is called Columbus Cove. It's one of the furthest beaches from the ship so it is typically less crowded than the beaches you pass to get here. You'll find the snorkeling by walking along the shore near the waterslide, toward the rocky coast. Go the opposite direction of all the beach chairs. Stick to the rocks along the shore and follow them out to the buoy line on the point. You should soon start to see more and more coral alongside multiple species of fish. This area is where the old tender pier was located. In fact, you can still see some remains from it including a large barrel and some chains located in the middle of the seagrass bed. Consider renting a floating mat for the day if you are not a strong swimmer or are worried about getting tired. Lay across the mat with your face in the water to get the views of snorkeling with the safety of a floatation device. Watch where you walk in this area as sea urchins are everywhere. Urchins are beautiful subjects for your underwater photographs, but they can ruin your day if you step on one.

While Labadee is the perfect beach day, take some time to walk the entire property. The sharp and rugged coastline is unlike most of the scenery throughout your trip. I highly recommend a walk out past the end of the zipline to Dragon's Lookout Point and Dragon's Breath Rock. Not only will this spot give you amazing views of Haiti, but if you listen closely you can hear the dragon breathing. The dragon exhales loudly as water moves in and out of the rocks. Just listen. It's unmistakable.

Labadee is a small port with lots to offer. Take time to explore!

COCO CAY

This private island in the Bahamas has, sadly, not caught up with the development of Labadee and is still a tender port. Think of the short ride in a smaller boat to the shore as a free excursion that everyone gets.

Coco Cay is another fantastic beach day. It has multiple beaches with free beach chairs. It also offers a variety of tours such as snorkeling and jet ski trips. The tour I got to participate in was the giant inflatable waterslide and aqua park. Both were way more fun than I had imagined and had me feeling like a kid again. You're on vacation; cut loose and be a little silly.

Remember to leave some time to explore the entire property. Coco Cay has a nature trail on the far edge and some of the best beaches are the furthest from the tender pier. Take time to look around. The best spots are not immediately visible.

SHOPPING

You won't find many shopping opportunities in the Private Destinations, but both Labadee and Coco Cay offer local craft markets. These markets are the only places on the property that require cash. The bars and tour operators will only accept your SeaPass card.

Like a lot of places in the Caribbean, look out for aggressive sales tactics. It's typical to hear a salesman call out to you and sometimes even run up to you and walk with you down the street trying to sell you something. It made me so uncomfortable in Labadee that I avoided going near the market altogether. There is another, longer, way through the center of the property, but it was worth it to me to walk in peace.

> BONUS ADVICE: I was a naive, sheltered American girl when I started my cruise ship adventures. I couldn't believe how friendly all the salesmen were in the islands. My thoughts were: "Wow! Everyone is so nice. They're all saying hello and asking me how I am. I guess I can stop and talk to them while I look in their store." That's their endgame. They're trying to get you to stop and shop. If you don't need anything and don't have time to waste, don't even acknowledge them. And most importantly, never stop moving your feet. You can say a quick "hello" if you feel rude not saying one, but stay the course! Always keep moving.

DINING

Since the Private Destinations are controlled and maintained by the ship, your options are limited. But the good news is that it's all included! Both Labadee and Coco Cay offer big lunch buffets with hamburgers, hot dogs, ribs, salad, pasta, rolls, cookies, and so much more. Water and fruit punch were offered free in both destinations with sodas and alcohol available for purchase. Check the map for your destination when you get off the ship as there may be multiple buffet locations. Avoid the closest one to the ship at noon as you'll almost certainly encounter a long line. Again, Columbus Cove in Labadee is your best bet for fewer crowds.

Keep an eye on your food as you walk from the buffet to wherever you choose to sit. I was walking away from the buffet in Coco Cay when a seagull swooped down and snatched the hot dog right out of the bun on my plate! I was mid-stride and he was mid-flight but managed to hit the moving target with precision. I had no other option but to watch in amazement as all the other seagulls gathered around the culprit and began fighting over my lunch.

If you're looking for a liquid lunch, keep an eye out for the ship's bar staff wandering the shores shouting "Labadoozie" and "Coco Loco." These specialty frozen drinks are available for purchase. They come virgin but the staff will add rum to it on the spot if requested. Each comes in a souvenir cup.

> BONUS ADVICE: The souvenir cup can come back on board, but the contents cannot. It must be consumed before you pass through security. Plan to purchase one with enough time to enjoy your drink. Some staff may try to sell to you while you are in line at the security checkpoint. They're doing their best to sell all of the drinks they have made, but don't pay for something you won't have time to enjoy.

PERFECT DAY

The Private Destinations offer an ideal day of relaxing on the beach. You don't have to find a taxi or a place to each lunch. Everything is accessible and included. Sit back, relax, and soak in the sun. If you decide you just can't sit still, go check out one of the tours. All of the tours will be available for purchase onboard, but also ashore. You can make a last minute decision and buy your ticket if you decide that the zipline or waterslide is calling your name.

BELOW DECK: AROUND THE WORLD

I've heard it said that the crew of a cruise ship is like a tiny United Nations. That statement is so true. I've never seen more people from more places come together to take care of business like a crew. I met and worked with people from all different countries who spoke all different languages. But we all had one thing in common: our ship. As crew for the same ship we were automatically family. It didn't matter if I knew them well or had just met them, they were my brothers and sisters.

Making friends was easy on the ship. Just by being there we all had something in common and we all had the shared goal of creating memorable vacations. I'm an introvert and typically take my time when making friends, but I made friends fast on the ship. And just as fast as you make them, they're gone. Turnover is constant for crew. When one crew member joins that means another one leaves. In some cases I became good friends with people just to have them leave a few weeks later. But there is always someone new and more friends to make. It is the oddest social environment ever, but it really works well.

I loved meeting people from other countries and learning about them and their cultures. We celebrated just about every country's independence day with a crew party. The parties typically featured food and music from the celebrated country. It was an amazing sight to see people celebrating their homes.

Working on a ship was like taking a trip around the world. There were always people to meet and something new to learn. We were more than just Indian, Jamaican, Mexican, Filipino, or American. We were crew. I say we turn control of the world over to a cruise ship's crew for a few months and see if we can't get to a better place.

CONCLUSION

I hope this book has provided some insight into the ports you will visit on your cruise vacation. Hopefully it has given you some practical advice and narrowed your options a bit. There is a lot to see in the Caribbean, but don't let the choices overwhelm you. The most important thing is that you create a vacation that is memorable and suitable for you.

Every cruise passenger is looking for something different. Some have come to relax and escape from work for a while. Some have come to spend quality time with their families. Others are looking for a grand adventure. Just as every person is different and unique, every cruise vacation will be different and unique.

While on your cruise, don't just soak up the sun. Take some time to really soak up the experience. For many of us, a cruise vacation is a splurge that we have worked long and hard to save for. Make time everyday to look around and take a deep breath of the ocean air. After that, take time to explore. Explore not only the ports of call, but also your ship. Try new things, see new sights, and make new friends. You will return home a richer person with a changed view of the world.

My goal for this book is not that you will visit every place I've listed or even all of my favorite places. My goal is that you are now inspired to explore wherever you are. I want all of us to live lives full of adventure and wonder. No one will experience the world in the same way you will, so it's up to each of us to make the most of everyday.

It's your life.

Go. Live.

BONUS ADVICE

All of the BONUS ADVICE from every chapter in one convenient location.

- Many of the ship's announcements won't come through the speaker in your stateroom. This way the PA won't disturb anyone who may be sleeping and you won't be inundated with information you simply don't care about. The announcements will be broadcast to all public areas, including the hallway outside your stateroom, so just crack the door open to listen.

- You can predict what type of demographic a cruise caters to based on its length. Long cruises (14 days or longer) will most likely host an older crowd: people who are retired and don't have to worry about pulling their kids out of school for a few weeks. The shortest cruises (3-4 days) will host the party crowd: people who are looking to get out of town for a long weekend and, in many cases, drink and party their worries away. Families heavily populate the medium length cruises (5-12 days) with a spike in attendance over the summer and around all of the school holidays. Of course, these can always vary, but keep this in mind when booking your trip.

- Stay on "Ship's Time." Ship's Time is the time it is onboard and this may or may not match what time it is on shore or even what time it is on other ships in the same port. If you are on a cruise sailing from Florida you are starting your vacation in the Eastern Time Zone. Some islands operate on Eastern time, but some operate on Atlantic time. To complicate matters further, this changes throughout the year. To simplify the process the cruise industry came up with the idea of "Ship's Time." When you first get onboard, check the time on the telephone in your stateroom and set your watch to match. This is the official time. Multiple announcements will be made if you ever need to adjust this time. It's always a good idea to double check the time on the ship's phone and the time on your watch before heading ashore to make sure you won't miss All On Board. Never rely on the time on your cell phone or ask a local for the time. I thankfully never missed the ship, but I was once late for work because I didn't observe Ship's Time.

- Pack light. Only take the essentials on your tour. Leave your phones, tablets, and non-waterproof cameras locked in your safe in your stateroom if you've booked a water based tour. On some tours I've had to leave everything in the van. At The Blue Hole in Jamaica we left everything in a pile steps from the road. On one visit part of the trail was washed out and we had to wade through the water to see the upper falls. We had no choice but to leave everything behind. For your own peace of mind, leave your valuables on board.

- When tendering, steer clear of peak times to avoid lines and get to shore or back to the ship quickly. For example, it's better to be on the first tender at 7:00 or 8:00. The busy times are 9:00 to 11:00 and you may encounter a wait. Similarly, plan to get back a couple hours early. Maybe book a spa treatment, spend some time at the pool, or enjoy a pre-dinner nap. Excursions frequently include a private tender to shore.

- Carry small bills with you on your tours. There will be many tipping opportunities. Come prepared. Your tour may also include a stop at a local craft or fruit market that you hadn't been expecting. Most of these places won't accept credit cards so having some cash on hand may get you a souvenir or a snack.

- No cooked food can be brought back onboard. Even if you just had the most amazing meal, don't buy another one and bring it with you. To this day, I still have it in my mind that I cannot take food back to my office. Really. It happened this week. You are clear to bring back packaged food. So buy all the souvenir taffy and chocolate you can carry.

- If you already know how to snorkel and plan on visiting more than one beach on your cruise vacation, I recommend buying your own mask and snorkel. You can find a set for $25.00 or less in the souvenir shops on the islands. Now you'll be prepared to snorkel anywhere your adventures take you. If you've never snorkeled before, consider booking a snorkeling excursion through your ship. Instruction is provided and the gear is supplied. It's a great way to literally get your feet wet and decide if snorkeling is a hobby for you.

- Carry cash! On my parents' first cruise we spent a day shopping in downtown Charlotte Amalie, St. Thomas. We had lots of time before All On Board so we decided to check out the Skyride to Paradise Point. We all had credit cards, but little cash, and the credit card machine was out of service. I left my parents to wander around Havensight Mall as I sprinted back to the ship, grabbed a handful of cash, and sprinted back outside to find them again. It all worked out and we loved our time at Paradise Point and still display pictures from that day in our homes. However, if we hadn't been so close to the ship we may have missed out or at least greatly cut short our time to explore. Come prepared for anything.

- I purchased an underwater digital camera from Royal Caribbean. I not only got a great deal, but it was probably the best purchase I ever made for life on a cruise ship. If you haven't bought one before your cruise, consider buying one in your first port. Many waterproof cameras are also freezeproof and shockproof. They are great for snorkel and river tubing trips as well as taking pictures in the rain without risking damage to your more expensive camera. Because of the camera's rugged exterior and shockproof quality, I used to clip mine to the waistbelt on my backpack while I was hiking. My camera has bounced off rocks on trails, been dropped numerous times, and still works great. If you plan on spending time in or under the water on your cruise, consider making this investment to capture those memories.

- Consider packing your favorite beverage for your cruise. While you're not allowed to bring alcohol onboard (any you purchase in port will be collected at the gangway and distributed to you before departure on the last day), I have seen people bring on cases of bottled water or their favorite soda. Your brand of choice may not be available where you are headed so consider bringing some with you.

- A tour that requires teamwork is a great way to make new

friends. My group was all crew members. I knew a few people, but most I had never spoken to. After sailing together for a few hours we all began saying hello to each other in the hallways and hanging out together in the Crew Bar. You will likely be on this tour with people you've never met before. After working together to sail your yacht, you'll have camaraderie with them that you won't share with other guests. This bond can create friendships that may last a lifetime.

- Renting scooters and ATVs in ports is dangerous. So dangerous your cruise line will likely discourage you from doing it. If you've never driven a scooter or an ATV, a highway in a foreign country is not a good place to start. However, if you're an experienced operator, I found that it was a great way to see the island. There is nothing separating you from your surroundings and you are free to go wherever you choose. That being said, I have seen people badly injured in accidents. Is seeing the island in this unique way worth the risk of road rash on your vacation?

- If someone offers to help you with your chair or umbrella, you will be expected to tip them. Early on in my career I naively thought they were just being friendly. In some spots I wasn't even allowed to rearrange the chairs on my own. If I started moving a chair, someone immediately showed up to "help" me.

- Go on a cruise to relax and spend time with those you love, not to watch sports. There is a decent chance that whatever team or sporting event you feel you must watch won't be shown on your ship. On the ships I was on we showed three NFL games on Sundays and the NFL chose which games we received. We couldn't get coverage of the Olympics, I never saw a hockey game, only select college games were shown, and Premier League soccer was blacked out. Literally. The channel would be playing as normal, it would say the game was about to start, and then the screen would go blank until the game ended. Sports leagues request enormous licensing fees for their games and some ships may not have the game you want. I once received a post cruise comment along the lines of, "I never would have come on this cruise if I had

known you wouldn't be showing the _____
game." If it's a game you absolutely must see, book your vacation in the off-season.

- Sometimes your peace of mind is worth the extra dollars you will spend on a tour. I was once left at a stop on a tour I booked on my own instead of through the ship. If I had been on the ship's tour they would have counted the guests before leaving each stop and realized I was missing.

- I was a naive, sheltered American girl when I started my cruise ship adventures. I couldn't believe how friendly all the salesmen were in the islands. My thoughts were: "Wow! Everyone is so nice. They're all saying hello and asking me how I am. I guess I can stop and talk to them while I look in their store." That's their endgame. They're trying to get you to stop and shop. If you don't need anything and don't have time to waste, don't even acknowledge them. And most importantly, never stop moving your feet. You can say a quick "hello" if you feel rude not saying one, but stay the course! Always keep moving.

- Souvenir cups can come back on board, but the contents cannot. It must be consumed before you pass through security. Plan to purchase one with enough time to enjoy your drink. Don't pay for something you won't have time to enjoy.

SAFETY TIPS

Just like anywhere, travel in the Caribbean can be dangerous. Nothing ruins a vacation faster than being robbed or victimized in some other way. But don't let any of this scare you, I never had any trouble. Here are a few tips to help keep you safe.

- Plan ahead. While I'm undoubtedly a huge fan of exploring, use common sense. Plan your route and if a street or neighborhood begins to make you feel uneasy, trust that feeling, and get back to where you feel comfortable.

- Try to not look like a tourist. Always walk with purpose and don't take out your map in public. Nothing screams, "I'm not from around here" louder than wandering about with a confused look on your face while holding a map.

- Travel in groups. I broke this rule constantly, but there is safety in numbers.

- Keep your wallet out of sight and out of reach. I always thought ahead about what I would be buying and tried to have just enough cash in my pocket for those items so I never needed to take my wallet out in public. I always took my wallet with me, but I stored it in the bottom of my backpack under a towel or sweatshirt so it was difficult to access. Guys, the worst thing you can do is carry your wallet in your back pocket. It's way too easy to snatch from there. At the very least, carry it in your front pocket.

- Leave your valuables behind. A beach is not a fashion show. Save your new diamond earrings and matching ring for formal night and avoid wearing them around in port.

- Don't talk to strangers. What your parents always told you is true. I found this especially true when I was exploring solo. I like to get a feel of local life so I ease up on this when in a group.

- Use common sense. Trust yourself and your instincts.

GLOSSARY

The cruise industry has it's own lingo. Here are a few words and phrases to help you be in the know as you set sail.

Arrival Time - Obviously this is the time your ship arrives in port. However, you typically cannot go ashore immediately. Allow some time for the gangways to be set and the ship's staff to complete the paperwork with the local port agent before you head down to exit. It's a great idea to go up to an outer deck to watch the sail in. After the ship has reached the pier and stopped moving, head back to your room, prepare for your day, and gather your things before going to the gangway.

Back Deck - The bar in the crew only area. Also called the Crew Bar.

Cruise Director or CD - The Director of Entertainment for the voyage. This person is responsible for all of your entertainment on board from the shows in the theater to games out on the pool deck. You will find him or her hosting events all around the ship everyday of your cruise. The Cruise Director will constantly be making announcements to let you know important information and what activities are happening where.

Disembark - Exit the ship. Staff will make announcements in ports of call notifying you of where you can disembark. Follow their directions if you want to get outside.

Embark - Board the ship. The first day of your cruise is called "Embarkation Day" and the port where you begin your cruise is called "Port of Embarkation."

Gangway - The ramp you walk across to get from the ship to the shore or vice versa.

Muster Drill or Assembly Drill - This is the one mandatory activity of your entire cruise and must take place within 24 hours of setting sail. When you hear seven short blasts, followed by one long blast on the ship's alarm bell system, you must go to the Emergency Station listed on your SeaPass card. Staff will be positioned throughout the ship to assist you in locating your spot. The Captain or Cruise Director will make announcements with further instructions.

Pilot - A specialist local to each port who comes on board to help the Captain and the Bridge Officers navigate the channel into port. He meets the ship on a pilot boat that pulls alongside your vessel. Your crew opens a set of doors (called a "shell gate") on a lower level and the pilot jumps in. Similarly, when leaving port, the pilot boat comes alongside and the pilot jumps from the ship to the boat.

Port Agent - A local worker in each port that coordinates the details of your ship's arrival and departure. Typically the Agent's or Agency's details are listed on your cruise documents. If the ship leaves without you in a port, the Port Agent will help you reconnect with the ship at the next port of call. Basically, you don't want to meet the Port Agent. Something has gone wrong if you do.

SeaPass Card - Room key and onboard credit card. It's the same size as a standard credit card or hotel room key. It will not only open your stateroom door, but you can charge drinks and souvenirs to it throughout the ship and in Private Destinations.

Ship's Time - The time it is onboard your vessel. It may or may not match the local time of the ports you visit. Check the clocks throughout the ship (including your stateroom telephone) to verify this time.

Staff or Staffy - Nickname for the Staff Captain, the second in command of the vessel. Some Staff Captains hate being called Staffy. Stick to Staff Captain.

Tender - A small boat that takes you from the ship to the shore when a pier is not available. Instead of docking, your ship will anchor offshore and a tender boat will ferry passengers back and forth.

THANKS

Thank you for reading my book!

I value your comments, feedback, and insights.

Together, we'll make the next version even better. Please leave a helpful review on Amazon.

Thanks again!

Valerie Perry

ABOUT THE AUTHOR

Now a passionate adventurer, Valerie Perry didn't grow up a traveler. She was the definition of a homebody and was too afraid to go to summer camp. Valerie received her college degree before her first boarding pass, but after seeing what was out there she has spent the last several years making up for lost time.

Valerie started her travel career touring North America with an organization called Silver Ring Thing. Then in October 2009, she headed out to sea as a Broadcast Technician for Royal Caribbean Cruise Lines. During her cruising career she lived on five ships: Explorer, Serenade, Jewel, Liberty, and Allure of the Seas. In 2013 she traded in her SeaPass card for a metrocard and moved to Washington, DC to begin a new chapter at National Geographic.

Nearly every step of her journey has been chronicled on her blog, The Road Lots Traveled which began as a way to share her stories of life on the road with her family back home. The blog has grown over the years and now features stories, photos, and videos from all across the United States, Scandinavia, the Mediterranean, and of course the Caribbean.

Readers frequently tell Valerie that they're living vicariously through her tales of adventure. While flattering, this motivates her to push harder and go farther. Valerie's mission is to inspire people to live larger, more passionate and adventurous lives than they ever dreamed possible. She believes that no one should have to live vicariously through her, or anyone else. She encourages her readers to take responsibility for their lives and live them well.

Valerie recently finished a quest to see 100 National Park Service sites before the National Park Service turned 100 on August 25, 2016. Follow her adventures on The Road Lots Traveled (www.theroadlotstraveled.com) and on Twitter and Instagram via @valeriedperry and #100by100.

Contact the author at valerie@theroadlotstraveled.com

Made in the
USA
Middletown, DE

75387024R00073